SYLLOGE NUMMORUM GRAECORUM

THE COLLECTION OF THE AMERICAN NUMISMATIC SOCIETY

THE AMERICAN NUMISMATIC SOCIETY
NEW YORK
1981

ISSN 0271-3993
ISBN 0-89722-187-7

COMPOSED IN BELGIUM AT CULTURA, WETTEREN
PRINTED BY THE MERIDEN GRAVURE COMPANY, MERIDEN, CONNECTICUT

PART 6

PALESTINE-SOUTH ARABIA

34. Ꭱ ↓ 3.82.
35. Ꭱ ↑ 3.99. Hirsch 24, 29 Nov. 1909 (Philipsen), 3067.

Obv. Janiform head (male? head l., female? head r.).
Rev. Forepart of horse r.; to upper l., Phoenician letter o = ᶜ (Gaza); all in incuse square with dotted border.
Obol.

36. Ꭱ ↓ 0.63. See *BMCPalestine*, p. 179, no. 20.

Obv. Bearded head r.
Rev. Janiform head (lion's head l., bearded head r.); to upper r., olive spray; all in incuse square with dotted border.
Drachm.

37. Ꭱ → 3.28. *Rev.* chisel cut. Newell 28.

Rev. Two monsters with lions' bodies, long necks, and bulls' heads, seated face to face; between them, facing mask; all in incuse square with cable border.
Drachm.

38. Ꭱ ↑ 3.37. *Rev.* chisel cut. See *BMCPalestine*, p. 181, no. 28.

Obv. Lion standing r. on back of crouching ram; above, Phoenician letter 𐤁 = B (see 11 above).
Rev. Bes standing facing, holding in outstretched arms two lions upside down with heads reverted; all in incuse square with dotted border.
Drachm.

39. Ꭱ ↗ 3.77 (holed). *Rev.* chisel cut. Newell 21.

Obv. Bearded head l.; to l., traces of uncertain inscription.
Drachm.

40. Ꭱ → 3.18. *Rev.* to r. and l. above, Phoenician inscription 𐤔𐤀 = ʼŠ; chisel cut. Abu Shusheh 1930 Hoard (*IGCH* 1507). Newell 20. Newell suggests that the reverse ʼŠ stands for ʼŠDOD (Ashdod). This now seems to be confirmed by another coin published in *Qadmoniot*, Israel Exploration Society (Jerusalem, Israel), vol. 9, nos. 2–3 (1976), p. 54, bearing the full name of the city, 𐤃𐤃𐤔𐤀 = ʼŠDD (Ashdod).

Obv. Facing head of Persian lion-griffin (?) in incuse square with dotted border.
Rev. Winged griffin seated r. in incuse square with dotted border.
Drachm.

41. Ꭱ → 3.10. Newell 32.

Obv. Bearded head of Bes, facing, in circular dotted border.
Rev. Lion's head r., in incuse square with dotted border.
Obol.

42. Ꭱ ↗ 0.72. Abu Shusheh 1930 Hoard (*IGCH* 1507). Newell 29 = Cahn 71, 14 Oct. 1931, 578.

Obv. Lion's head, facing.
Rev. Same type, in incuse square.
Hemiobol.

43. Ꭱ ← 0.25.

Obv. Helmeted male head r.
Rev. Two lions seated facing each other; below, two dolphins facing each other; all in incuse square with dotted border.
Obol.

44. Ꭱ ↑ 0.64. Abu Shusheh 1930 Hoard (*IGCH* 1507). Newell 30 = Cahn 71, 14 Oct. 1931, 576. A similar rev. type on a larger denomination (drachm) with Phoenician or Aramaic letter "B" has been published by Y. Meshorer, "An Unusual Coin of the Persian Period," *Israel Museum News* 9 (1972), pp. 78–80.

Obv. Male head r., in circular dotted border.
Rev. Ibex standing r., head reverted; on his back, small falcon; all in incuse square with dotted border.
Obol.

45. Ꭱ ↓ 0.67. Newell 31 = Cahn 71, 14 Oct. 1931, 577. Possibly struck at Ashdod, as a similar ibex is depicted on the coin of Ashdod published in the reference cited under 40 above.

Obv. Male figure in Persian costume standing r., holding bridle of facing horse; to l., Phoenician inscription 𐤋𐤔 = ŠL; all in incuse square with dotted border.
Rev. Lion standing r., head reverted; to l., 𐤋𐤔 = ŠL; below, ram's head; all in incuse square with dotted border.
Obol.

46. Ꭱ ↑ 0.83. Newell 23.

Obv. Lion seated l., head facing; to r., Phoenician inscription 𐤋𐤔 = ŠL; all in incuse square with dotted border.
Rev. Lion advancing l., head facing; to r., 𐤋𐤔 = ŠL; all in incuse square with dotted border.
Obol.

47. Ꭱ → 0.60. Newell 24.

Obv. Facing female (?) head in circular dotted border.
Rev. Facing head of Bes wearing crown of feathers; all in shallow incuse circle.
See *BMCPalestine*, p. 182, nos. 1–3.
Obols.

48. Ꭱ ↓ 0.61.
49. Ꭱ ↘ 0.83. Ex Pozzi coll.
50. Ꭱ ↖ 0.69. Ex Pozzi coll.

A. GRECO-PALESTINIAN COINS

These coins, of the fourth century B.C., are grouped by types rather than by mints. Newell references are to the individual coins in E. T. Newell, *Miscellanea Numismatica: Cyrene to India*, NNM 82 (New York, 1938).

Obv. Head of Athena r., wearing crested Attic helmet adorned with olive leaves. Athena's eye frontal (1–4), and profile (5–13).
Rev. ΑΘΕ Owl standing r.; to l., olive spray and crescent; all in shallow incuse square (sometimes not preserved).
Tetradrachms (1–4) and drachms (5–14).

1. Æ ↑ 17.19. *Obv.* Archaic style. *Rev.* no ΑΘΕ; to l. and r., Phoenician inscription ʅΘ = ᶜZ (Gaza); owl stands facing, flanked by two olive sprays; all in shallow incuse square. Tell el Maskhuta 1947–48 Hoard (*IGCH* 1649). Struck at Gaza, ca. 400 B.C.
2. Æ ← 13.68. *Obv.* style inferior. *Rev.* to lower r., facing lion's head. This interesting and hitherto unpublished issue was apparently struck at either Tyre or Gaza, since both cities minted coins depicting a lion's head.
3. Æ ← 16.52. *Obv.* on cheek, Hebrew-Samaritan-Aramaic letter ⩒ = Š. This coin and 4–10 below may have been struck in the Samaritan city of Shomron, if Š stands for Shomron.
4. Æ ← 16.38. *Obv.* on cheek, countermark: Hebrew-Samaritan-Aramaic letter ⩒ = Š. *Rev.* to r., countermark: Aramaic letter 𐡌 = M, in rectangular incuse; two chisel cuts. This coin is apparently from the mint of Athens, but is included here because of the two countermarks, Š (standing for Shomron?), and M (standing apparently for Mazdai, the Persian governor of Cilicia).
5. Æ ↖ 4.25. *Rev.* to r., Hebrew-Samaritan-Aramaic letter ⩒ = Š. Cilicia before 1914 Hoard (*IGCH* 1259); it is possible that 6–10 below derive from the same hoard, although the record does not indicate this. Struck at Shomron(?), ca. 350 B.C.
6. Æ ↑ 4.19. As 5.
7. Æ ↑ 4.24. As 5.
8. Æ ← 4.30. As 5.
9. Æ ↓ 4.31. As 5.
10. Æ ↑ 4.20. As 5.
11. Æ ↑ 4.17. *Obv.* on cheek, Aramaic letter 𐡁 = B. Many of the so-called Philisto-Arabian coins have the Aramaic letter B on the cheek. Newell suggests (pp. 50–51) that it stands for Batis (or Babenesis), the governor of Gaza just before Alexander's conquest. Thus, it is likely that this coin was struck at Gaza in the third quarter of the fourth century B.C.
12. Æ → 4.24. *Obv.* on cheek, Aramaic letter ʋ = ᶜ (probably for Gaza).
13. Æ ↓ 3.95. *Obv.* raised oval without type.
14. Æ → 4.46. *Obv.* uncertain head of crude style l. *Rev.* no ΑΘΕ; owl stands l.; to l., uncertain Semitic inscription; all in shallow incuse circle.

Obv. Head of Athena r., with profile eye, wearing crested Attic helmet adorned with olive leaves (15–19, 21, 23–24, 27–28), youthful male head r., wearing taenia (20), raised oval, representing head? (22), female head r., wearing Oriental headdress (25), helmeted male head r. (26), head of Athena wearing Corinthian helmet (29), or Phoenician galley l. (30).
Rev. ΑΘΕ Owl standing r.; to l., on most coins, olive spray; all in shallow incuse square (sometimes not preserved).
Obols (15–19, 22–30) and hemiobols (20–21).

15. Æ ↑ 0.61. *Rev.* to r., letter 𐤌 = M (mintmark of Gaza).
16. Æ ← 0.52. As 15, but no ΑΘΕ.
17. Æ → 0.77. *Obv.* to r., Phoenician letter ο = ᶜ (Gaza?).
18. Æ ← 0.80. Nablus region 1968 Hoard (*IGCH* 1504).
19. Æ ↑ 0.74. Nablus region 1968 Hoard (*IGCH* 1504).
20. Æ ← 0.32. Abu Shusheh 1930 Hoard (*IGCH* 1507). Newell 27 = Cahn 71, 14 Oct. 1931, 574.
21. Æ → 0.34. *Rev.* to r., Phoenician letter ο = ᶜ (Gaza?).
22. Æ ↑ 0.86. *Rev.* to r., uncertain Semitic inscription. Nablus region 1968 Hoard (*IGCH* 1504).
23. Æ ← 0.66. *Rev.* to r., Palaeo-Hebrew inscription 𐤋𐤌𐤁 (?) = NML (?) Nablus region 1968 Hoard (*IGCH* 1504).
24. Æ ← 0.74. *Rev.* to r., Aramaic inscription 𐡕𐡍𐡃𐡌. Abu Shusheh 1930 Hoard (*IGCH* 1507). Newell 25. Another Abu Shusheh coin from the rev. die of 24 has been published by Lambert, *QDAP* 2 (1933), p. 5, no. 4. Newell suggests reading the Aramaic inscription as MNFT, which has no meaning at all. We suggest that the reading should be TDNM-*Datames*, retrograde. See *BMCLycaonia*, pp. 167–68.
25. Æ → 0.75. *Rev.* no ΑΘΕ; to r., Phoenician inscription 𐤍𐤀 = 'N. The inscription may stand for Ascalon, A and N being the first and last letters of the name of the city. See *BMCPalestine*, p. 177, no. 4.
26. Æ ↖ 0.55. *Rev.* ₣ replaces ΑΘΕ. Nablus region 1968 Hoard (*IGCH* 1504).
27. Æ ↖ 0.87. *Rev.* no ΑΘΕ; to r., lily blossom and traces of uncertain Aramaic inscription. Overstruck. Newell 26. Newell describes the flower on rev. as "lotus bud."
28. Æ ↑ 0.53. *Rev.* to r., Egyptian hieroglyph 𓊽. Newell 33. Newell describes the sign as *uah* (durability).
29. Æ ↑ 0.57. *Rev.* no. ΑΘΕ; to l. and r., Egyptian hieroglyphs 𓎛 and 𓂋 ; to r., lotus flower. Newell 34. Newell reads the hieroglyphs as a garbled ΑΘΕ.
30. Æ ↑ 0.66 (holed). *Obv.* above, Phoenician letter 𐤁 = B. *Rev.* ΑΘΕ to l. Newell 22. With regard to the B, see 11 above. Newell suggests that the rev. inscription should read OF.

Obv. Janiform head (bearded head l., female head r.).
Rev. Owl standing r., flanked by two ears of corn; to lower r., Phoenician inscription 𐤆𐤆𐤏 = ᶜZH (Gaza); all within incuse square.
Drachm.

31. Æ ↑ 3.91. See *BMCPalestine*, p. 176, no. 1.

Obv. Female head r.
Rev. Owl standing facing, wings spread; to upper l., inscription 𐤍𐤀 = 'N (Ascalon?, see 25 above); all in incuse square.
Drachm.

32. Æ ↓ 3.41. See *BMCPalestine*, p. 177, nos. 8–9.

Obv. Bearded head r.
Rev. Forepart of horse r.; to upper l., Phoenician inscription 𐤏𐤆 = ᶜZ (Gaza); all in incuse square with dotted border.
Drachms.

33. Æ ↑ 3.50. *Rev.* chisel cut. For 33–35, see *BMCPalestine*, p. 178, no. 14.

TRANSLITERATION SYSTEM

	HEBREW				ARAMAIC		
TRANSLITERATION	MODERN HEBREW	HASMONAEAN	JEWISH WAR	BAR-COCHBA	HASMONAEAN	NABATAEAN	SABAEAN
ʾ		[illegible]	[illegible]	[illegible]	[illegible]	[illegible]	[illegible]
ʿ			[illegible]	[illegible]		[illegible]	[illegible]
B B̲	בּ ב	[illegible]	[illegible]	[illegible]		[illegible]	[illegible]
D	דּ	[illegible]	[illegible]		[illegible]	[illegible]	[illegible]
D̲	ד						[illegible]
G	ג	[illegible]	[illegible]	[illegible]		[illegible]	
H	ה	[illegible]	[illegible]	[illegible]	[illegible]	[illegible]	[illegible]
Ḥ	ח	[illegible]	[illegible]	[illegible]		[illegible]	[illegible]
K	כּ	[illegible]		[illegible]	[illegible]	[illegible]	[illegible]
K̲	כ/ך	[illegible]				[illegible]	
L	ל	[illegible]	[illegible]	[illegible]	[illegible]	[illegible]	[illegible]
M	מ/ם	[illegible]	[illegible]	[illegible]	[illegible]	[illegible]	[illegible]
N	נ/ן	[illegible]	[illegible]	[illegible]	[illegible]	[illegible]	[illegible]
P	פּ					[illegible]	
P̲	פ/ף					[illegible]	[illegible]
Q	ק		[illegible]			[illegible]	
R	ר	[illegible]	[illegible]	[illegible]	[illegible]	[illegible]	[illegible]
Ś	שׂ		[illegible]	[illegible]			
Š	שׁ	[illegible]	[illegible]	[illegible]	[illegible]	[illegible]	[illegible]
S	ס				[illegible]	[illegible]	[illegible]
Ṣ	צ/ץ		[illegible]			[illegible]	[illegible]
T	ת	[illegible]	[illegible]	[illegible]	[illegible]	[illegible]	[illegible]
Ṭ	ט					[illegible]	
W	ו	[illegible]	[illegible]	[illegible]	[illegible]	[illegible]	[illegible]
Y	י	[illegible]	[illegible]	[illegible]		[illegible]	[illegible]
Z	ז			[illegible]			

PREFACE

The sixth fascicule in the American Numismatic Society's contribution to the series Sylloge Nummorum Graecorum is concerned with the geographical area consisting of ancient Palestine, the Decapolis, Provincia Arabia, Nabataea, and South Arabia. The catalogue has been prepared by Ya'akov Meshorer whose arrangement of the coinage has been followed here. The photographs, all taken directly from the coins, were made by Michael Di Biase.

The vast majority of coins from Palestine and Arabia at the ANS originally formed the collection of Edward T. Newell. While this collection is not one of the largest in the world, Newell chose well to make it one of the most important of its kind, containing issues that are often rare, if not unique. As will be noted in the catalogue, Newell acquired a few specimens from the Pozzi collection that did not appear in the Naville 1, 1921, sale.

The material in this volume is arranged as follows:

	Nos.
A. GRECO-PALESTINIAN COINS, 4th cent. B.C.	1–50
B. JEWISH COINS	
Yehud, 4th–3rd cent. B.C.	51–52
Hasmonaean, 103–37 B.C.	53–194
Herodian, 40 B.C.–A.D. 95	195–320
Roman Procurators, A.D. 6–62	321–418
Jewish War against Rome, A.D. 66–70	419–61
Judaea Capta and Roman Administration, A.D. 81–96	462–500
Bar Cochba War, A.D. 132–35	501–92
C. PROVINCIAL CITY COINS	593–1118
D. COINS OF THE DECAPOLIS AND PROVINCIA ARABIA	1119–1420
E. NABATAEAN COINS, 84 B.C.–A.D. 106	1421–52
F. SOUTH ARABIAN COINS, 3rd cent. B.C.–1st cent. A.D.	1453–1615
G. INDICES	
1. Geographical	
2. Rulers, Princes and Governors	
3. Obverse Types	
4. Reverse Types	
5. Secondary Symbols and Mintmarks	
6. Countermarks	
7. Hoards	
8. Overstrikes	

Included in this volume are two mints which have previously been assigned to the geographical area of Trachonitis : Caesarea Panias and Gaba. Caesarea Panias is certainly the same city and mint founded by the Jewish ruler Herod Philip, who struck Jewish coinage there, as did Agrippa II later. Gaba is apparently to be associated with a city situated near Megiddo, in the Jezreel valley, at the foot of Mount Carmel. Most of the coins minted in Gaba were discovered in this vicinity.

Because of the system of organization, the following subdivision of coins from certain mints is employed:

1. Tiberias : Jewish coins of Herod Antipas and Herod Agrippa I are described in section B.
2. Caesarea : Jewish coins of Herod Agrippa I and Agrippa II, and Judaea Capta coins are described in section B.
3. Caesarea Panias: Jewish coins of Herod Philip and Agrippa II are described in section B.
4. Gaza: Early coins from Gaza, dated before the conquests of Alexander the Great, are described in section A.
5. Petra: The coins struck in Petra by the Nabataeans are described in section E.
6. Since the coins of Aretas III are an integral part of Nabataean coinage, they are included in this volume even though they were minted in Damascus.

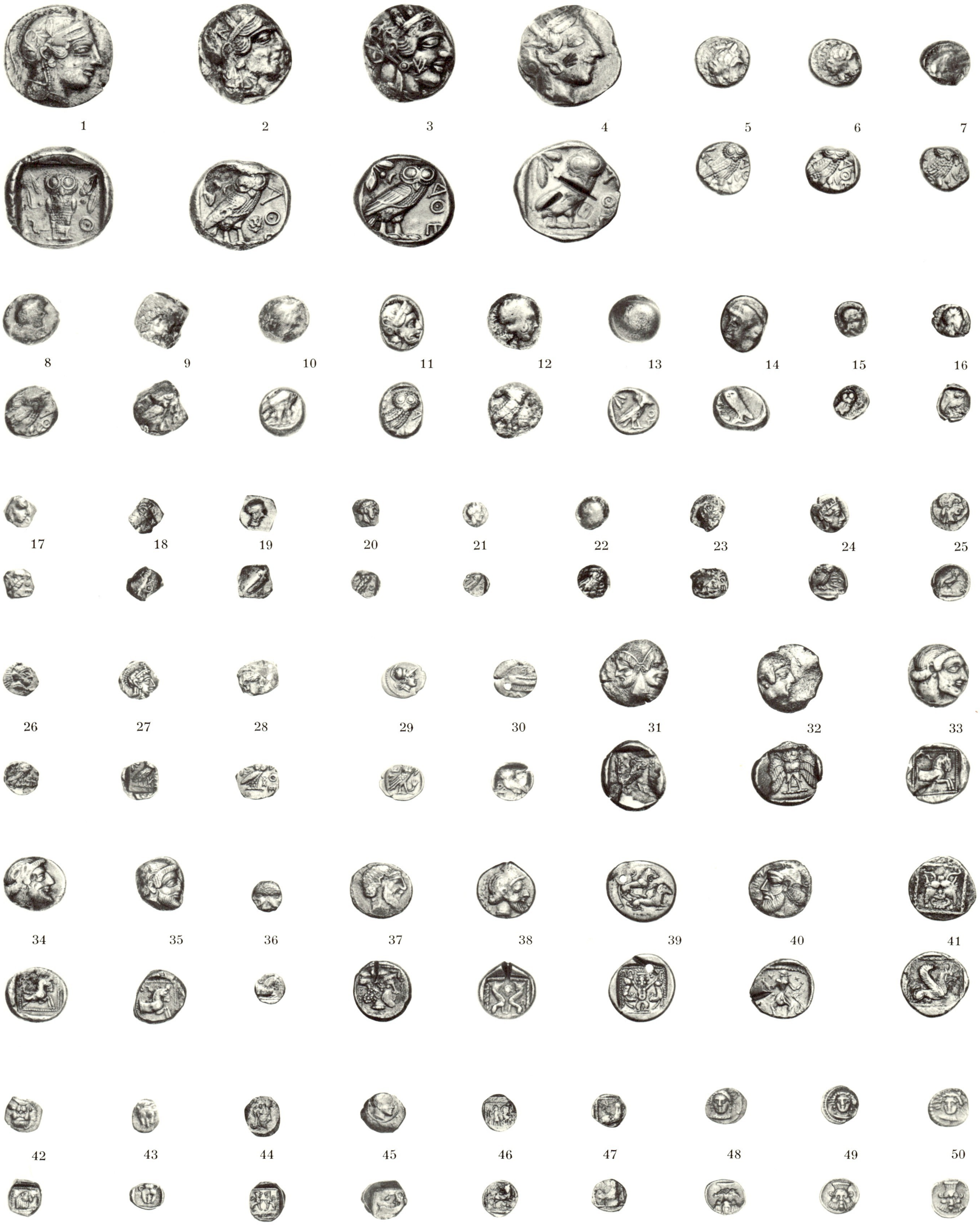
1 2 3 4 5 6 7
8 9 10 11 12 13 14 15 16
17 18 19 20 21 22 23 24 25
26 27 28 29 30 31 32 33
34 35 36 37 38 39 40 41
42 43 44 45 46 47 48 49 50

51 51 (enlarged) 52 (enlarged) 52

53 54 55 56 57 58 59

60 61 62 63 64 65 66

67 68 69 70 71 72 73

74 75 76 77 78 79 80

81 82 83 84 85 86 87

B. JEWISH COINS: YEHUD

INS references are to the individual coins in Israel Numismatic Society, *The Dating and Meaning of Ancient Jewish Coins and Symbols. Six Essays in Jewish Numismatics.* Numismatic Studies and Researches 2 (Tel Aviv/Jerusalem, 1958).

Time of Persian Rule (ca. 350 B.C.)
Mint of Jerusalem

Obv. Head of Athena r., of crude style.
Rev. Palaeo-Hebrew inscription = YHD (Yehud, the name of the Province of Judaea under Persian rule). Owl standing r.; to l., lily flower.
Obol.

51. AR ↓ 0.50. Found south of Jerusalem. Published by L. Mildenberg, *Essays Thompson*, p. 193, no. 7.

Time of the Ptolemies (*Ptolemy I or II*)

Obv. Diademed head of Ptolemy I r.
Rev. Palaeo-Hebrew inscription = YHD[H] (Yehuda). Eagle standing l.
Tetartemorion.

52. AR ↑ 0.185. Published by L. Mildenberg, *Essays Thompson*, p. 195, no. 25.

HASMONAEAN

For the recent downdating of the beginning of Hasmonaean coinage, now generally accepted, see Y. Meshorer, "The Beginning of the Hasmonean Coinage," *IEJ* 24 (1974), pp. 59–61.

Alexander Jannaeus (103–76 B.C.)
Mint of Jerusalem

Obv. ΑΛΕΞΑΝΔΡΟΥ ΒΑΣΙΛΕΩΣ (sometimes incompletely preserved). Anchor, surrounded by diadem (53–54).
Rev. Palaeo-Hebrew inscription = YHWNTN HMLK̲ (Yehonatan the King). Lily flower.

53. Æ ← 2.69.
54. Æ → 2.38.

Rev. Palaeo-Hebrew inscription (sometimes incompletely preserved) = Y.H.WN. T.N.H.ML.K̲ (Yehonatan the King) between rays of eight-rayed star; all surrounded by diadem.

55. Æ ↑ 3.04.
56. Æ ↑ 2.64.
57. Æ ↑ 2.54.
58. Æ ↑ 2.21.
59. Æ ↑ 2.38.
60. Æ ↑ 2.14. *INS* 2.
61. Æ ↑ 2.51.
62. Æ ↑ 3.08.
63. Æ ↑ 2.26.
64. Æ ↑ 3.04.
65. Æ ↙ 2.64.
66. Æ ↓ 3.57.
67. Æ ↓ 3.06.
68. Æ ↓ 2.26.
69. Æ ↑ 1.78.
70. Æ ↑ 1.29. *Rev.* inscription Y.N.T.N.H.M.L.K.
71. Æ ↑ 1.21.
72. Æ ↑ 2.09. Crude style. *Obv.* ΒΑΣΙΛΕΩ ΑΛΣΑVΟ *Rev.* Y.H.N.TN.M.L. ...
73. Æ ↑ 1.19. Crude style; inscriptions poorly preserved and garbled.
74. Æ ↑ 1.84. As 73.
75. Æ ↑ 1.29. As 73.
76. Æ ↑ 2.11. As 73.

Obv. ΑΛΕΞΑΝΔΡΟΥ ΒΑΣΙΛΕΩΣ (sometimes incompletely preserved). Anchor surrounded by broad circle.
Rev. Aramaic inscription (sometimes incompletely preserved) = MLK' 'LKSNDRS ŠNT KH (of King Alexander, year 25). Eight-rayed star within dotted circle.

77. Æ ↑ 0.80. *Obv.* to l. and r. of anchor, crudely rendered LKE (78 B.C.).
78. Æ ↑ 1.48. *Obv.* as 77.
79. Æ 1.11. *Obv.* as 77.
80. Æ 1.77. *Obv.* as 77.
81. Æ 0.80. *Obv.* as 77.
82. Æ 1.50. *Obv.* as 77.
83. Æ 1.25.
84. Æ 1.42.
85. Æ 1.04.
86. Æ 1.56.
87. Æ 0.97.

JEWISH COINS: HASMONAEAN

Alexander Jannaeus, Jerusalem (cont.)

88. Æ 0.75. Small crude flan.
89. Æ 1.04. As 88.
90. Æ 0.72. As 88.
91. Æ 1.06. As 88.
92. Æ 0.87. As 88.
93. Æ 0.87. Small, very crude flan. *Rev.* star has six rays.
94. Æ 0.78. As 93.
95. Æ 0.69. As 93.
96. Æ 0.62. As 93.

Obv. Palaeo-Hebrew inscription

(Yehonatan the High Priest and the Hever [Council] of the Jews); all within wreath.
Rev. Double cornucopiae; in center, pomegranate.

97. Æ ↑ 1.42. *Obv.* inscription as given in heading = YHW / NTNHK / HNHGDLW / ḤBRHY / DM.
98. Æ ↘ 2.02. *Obv.* YHW / NTNHK / HNHGD / LWḤḆ.
99. Æ ↑ 2.27. *Obv.* YHW / NTNHK / HNHGDL / WḤḆRH / YDY.
100. Æ ↘ 2.08. *Obv.* YHW / NTNHK / HNHGD / LḤḆRH / YHD.
101. Æ ↓ 1.91. *Obv.* YHW / NTNHK / HNHGDL / ḤBRH.
102. Æ ↑ 2.37. *Obv.* YHW / NTNHK / HNHGDL / ḤḆRH / DM.
103. Æ ↙ 2.08. *Obv.* YHW / NTNHK / HNHGD / LWḤḆ.
104. Æ ↓ 1.21. *Obv.*]KHNH / GDLWḤ / RYH.
105. Æ ↓ 1.45. *Obv.* YHW / NTNH / KHNHG / LWḤḆR / YD.
106. Æ ↑ 1.74. *Obv.* YH / NTNH /]HGD[/ ḆR.

Obv. As 97, but with different style of script

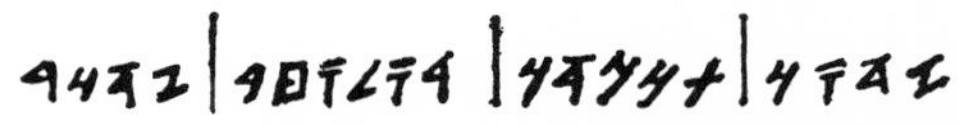

107. Æ ↑ 1.68. *Obv.* inscription as giving in heading = YHWN / TNKHN / DWLḤḆ / YHWD.
108. Æ ↑ 1.58. *Obv.* YHWN / TNHKG / DWLWḤḆ / YHW.
109. Æ ↑ 2.38. *Obv.* YHWN / TNKHG / DWLḤḆ / RYHW / DM.
110. Æ ↙ 1.82. *Obv.* YHWN / TNHKH / DWLWḤḆ / RYH.
111. Æ ↙ 1.68. *Obv.* YWHN / THKHN / DWLWḤB / HYHW.
112. Æ ↑ 2.18. *Obv.* YHWN / TNHK / DWLWḤḆ / HYH.
113. Æ ↘ 2.31. *Obv.* YHWN / TNKH / DWLḤḆ / YH.
114. Æ ↑ 1.76. *Obv.* YHWN / TNHKH / HGDWLḤ / RYH.
115. Æ ↓ 2.10. *Obv.* YHWN / TNHK / DLḤ / [.

Obv. As 97, but with different style of script

 = YHWNT / NKH·NGD / LWḤḆR / YHWD / M.

116. Æ ↓ 2.07.

Obv. As 97, but with different style of script

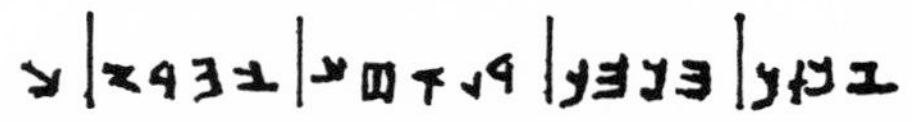

117. Æ ↙ 2.50. *Obv.* inscription as given in heading = YNTN / HKHN / DLWḤḆ / YHDY / M.
118. Æ ↑ 1.90. *Obv.* YNTN / KHNDL / WḤḆR / YHD.
119. Æ ↙ 2.00. *Obv.* YNTN / KHNGDLW / ḤBRY / HDYM.
120. Æ ↗ 1.97. *Obv.* YNTNH / KHNGDL / WḤḆRY / HDYM.
121. Æ ↗ 1.66. *Obv.* YNTN / DKHN / LḤḆ / RYD.
122. Æ → 2.29. *Obv.* YNTN / HKN G / DWLWḤḆ / HYHDY.
123. Æ ↗ 1.71. *Obv.* YNTN / [ ] / WḤḆR / YHDY.

Obv. As 97, but with the name of the king shortened from YHWNTN to YNTN.
Nos. 124–34 are overstruck on the issue of nos. 53–54 above. Traces of the undertypes are noted where identifiable.

124. Æ ↓ 1.94. *Obv.* YNT / NHKH / HGDLW / ḤḆR; traces of anchor and Greek inscription, ΔΡΟΥ Β. *Rev.* traces of lily.
125. Æ ↑ 1.77. *Obv.* YNTN / HKHNH / GDLW / ḆR; traces of lily. *Rev.* traces of anchor and Greek inscription, ΥΒΑΣΙΛΕ.
126. Æ ↑ 2.12. *Obv.* YNTN / KHNH LWḤ / HD; traces of anchor and Greek inscription, Ε ΞΑ. *Rev.* traces of lily and Hebrew inscription, NTNHMLK.
127. Æ ↑ 2.48. *Obv.* YNTN / HKHN / GDLWḤ / RYH. *Rev.* traces of diadem around anchor and Greek inscription, ΒΑΣΙΛΕΩΣ.
128. Æ ↑ 1.67. *Obv.* YNTN / HKHNH / GDLWḤ / Y.
129. Æ ↙ 2.92. *Obv.* YNTN / HKHNH / GDLWḤḆ / RYHD.

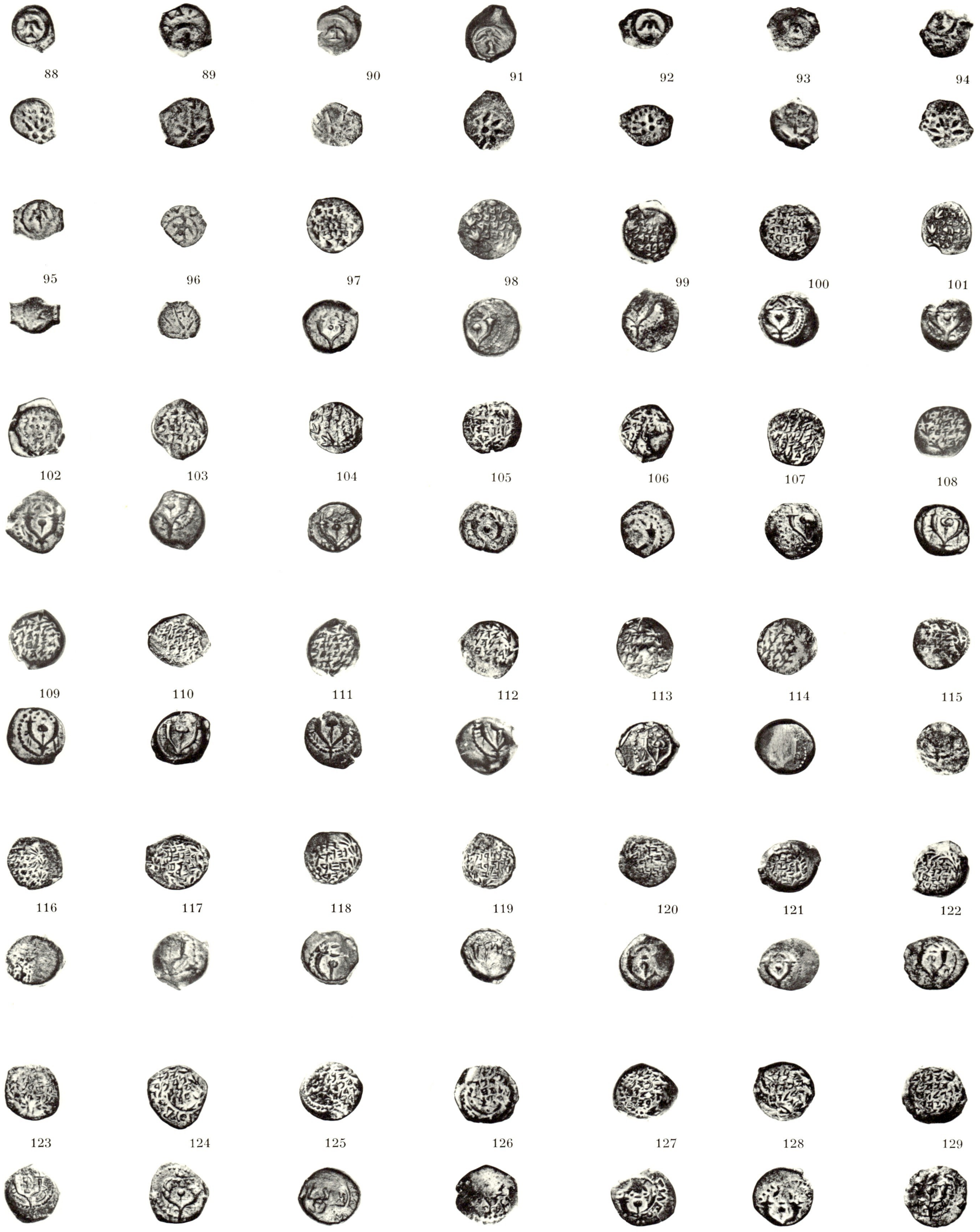

88 89 90 91 92 93 94

95 96 97 98 99 100 101

102 103 104 105 106 107 108

109 110 111 112 113 114 115

116 117 118 119 120 121 122

123 124 125 126 127 128 129

130 131 132 133 134 135 136 137
138 139 140 141 142 143 144 145
146 147 148 149 150 151 152 153
154 155 156 157 158 159 160 161
162 163 164 165 166 167 168 169
170 171 172 173 174 175 176 177

JEWISH COINS: HASMONAEAN

Alexander Jannaeus, Jerusalem (cont.)

130. Æ ↓ 2.05. *Obv.* YNTN / HKHN / GDLWḤ / ḆRY.
131. Æ ↑ 3.05. *Obv.* YNTN / HKHN / GDLWḤ / Y.
132. Æ ↑ 2.52. *Obv.* YNT[/ HKHN / GDLWḤ / RYH.
133. Æ ↗ 2.62. *Obv.* YNTN / KHN / GD / [.
134. Æ ↑ 1.96. *Obv.* YNTN / HKHN / GDLWḤ / RH.

Judas Aristobulus II (67–63 B.C.)
Mint of Jerusalem

Obv. Palaeo-Hebrew inscription

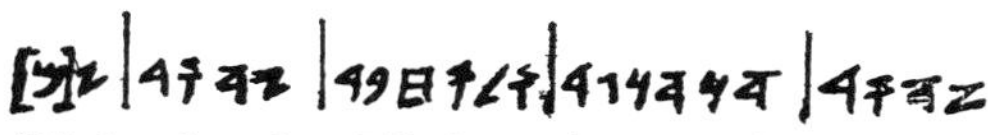

(Yehuda the High Priest and the Council of the Jews); all within wreath.
Rev. Double cornucopiae; in center, pomegranate.

135. Æ ↗ 1.83. *Obv.* inscription as given in heading = YHWD / HKHNGD / WLWḤḆR / YHWD / YM.
136. Æ ↗ 2.63. *Obv.* YHWD / HKHNGD / WLWḤḆRH / YHWD / YM.
137. Æ ↗ 1.94. *Obv.* YHWD / HKHNGD / WLWḤḆ / YH.
138. Æ ↗ 1.87. *Obv.* YHWD / HKHNGD / WLWḤḆR / YHW.

John Hyrcanus II (63–40 B.C.)
Mint of Jerusalem

Obv. Palaeo-Hebrew inscription

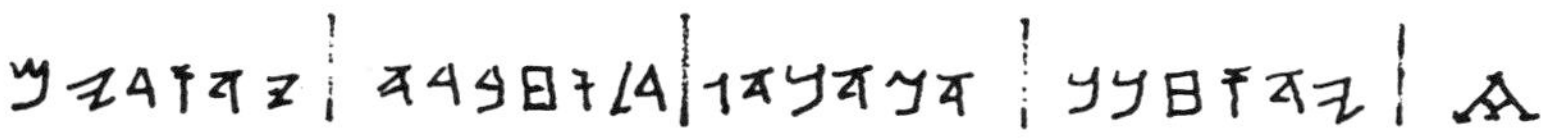

(Yehoḥanan the High Priest and the Council of the Jews); all within wreath.
Rev. Double cornucopiae; in center, pomegranate.

139. Æ ↑ 1.41. *Obv.* inscription as given in heading = YHWḤNN / HKHNHG / DLWḤḆRH / YHWDYM; above, Greek letter Α.
140. Æ ↑ 2.09. *Obv.* YHWḤNN / HKHNHGD / LWḤḆRHY / HWDYM; above, Greek letter Α, *INS* 3.
141. Æ ↖ 1.47. *Obv.* YHWḤNN / HKHNHG / DLWḤḆR / HYHWDYM; above, Greek letter Α.
142. Æ ↗ 2.20. *Obv.* YHWḤNN / HKHNHGD / LWḤḆRHY / HWDYM; above, Greek letter Α.
143. Æ ↗ 2.26. *Obv.* YHWḤNN / HKHNHGD / LWḤḆRHY / HWDYM; above, Greek letter Α.

Obv. As 139, but with different style of script and small change of text

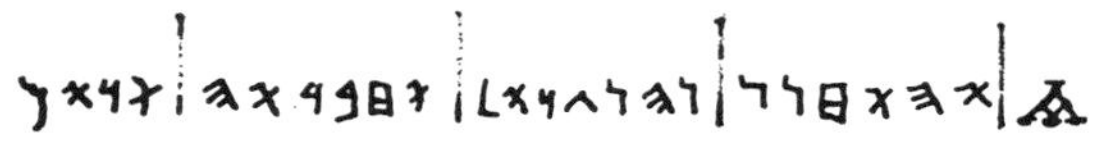

(Yehoḥanan High Priest and Council of Jews [*sic*]).

144. Æ ↗ 2.39. *Obv.* inscription as given in heading = YHWḤNN / KHNGDWL / WḤḆRYH / WDYM; above, Greek letter Α.
145. Æ ↑ 2.47. As 144.

Obv. As 139, but with different style of script

146. Æ ↗ 1.87. *Obv.* inscription as given in heading = YHWḤNNH / KHNGDL / WḤḆRHY / HDYM.
147. Æ ↑ 2.60. *Obv.* YHWḤN / NHKHNH / GDLWḤḆR / HYHDY / M.
148. Æ ↑ 1.57. *Obv.* YHWḤNN / HKHNHG / DLWḤḆR / HYHD / YM.
149. Æ ↑ 2.23. *Obv.* YHWḤNN / HKHNHG / DLHḤḆR / HYHD.
150. Æ ↑ 1.64. *Obv.* apparently due to a spelling mistake during the production of the die, the second word in the second line was deleted and the inscription was renewed in the third line: YHWḤNN / HKHN[[ ]] / HGDLWḤ / ḆRHYH / DYM. *Rev.* to l., Greek monogram ⩎.
151. Æ ↑ 2.34. *Obv.* inscription garbled: YHWḤNN / HKHNHG / DLHYHD / HYHD / YM (Yehoḥanan the High Priest the Jews the Jews). *Rev.* as 150.
152. Æ ↑ 2.07. *Obv.* YHWḤNN / HKHNHG / DLWḤḆR / HYHD. *Rev.* as 150.
153. Æ ↑ 2.76. *Obv.* YHWḤNN / HKHNHG / DLHḤḆR / HY *Rev.* to l. Greek letter Π
154. Æ ↑ 1.85. *Obv.* YHWḤN / NHKHNH / GDLWḤḆR / YHW. *Rev.* to l., Greek letter Α.
155. Æ ↑ 2.20. *Obv.* YHWḤNN / HKHNHG / DLWḤḆR / HYHD / YM.
156. Æ ↑ 2.20. *Obv.* YHWḤNN / HKHNHG / DLWḤḆR / HYHD / M.
157. Æ ↑ 1.77. *Obv.* YHWḤNN / HKHNHG / DLWḤḆRH / YHDYM. *Rev.* as 154.
158. Æ ↑ 1.44. *Obv.* YHWḤNN / HKHN / GDLHḤ[/ .Y. . *Rev.* to l., Greek letter Λ(Α?).
159. Æ ↑ 2.08. *Obv.* YHWḤN[N] / HKHNHGḌ / LWḤḆRH / YHDYM. *Rev.* as 158.
160. Æ ↗ 2.71. *Obv.* YH / WḤNNH / KHNHGDL / WḤḆRH / YHWD. *Rev.* to r., Greek letter Δ
161. Æ ↑ 1.84. *Obv.* YHWḤNN / HKHNHG / DLHḤḆR / HYHD / M.
162. Æ ↑ 2.18. *Obv.* YHWḤNN / HKHNHG / DLHḤḆR / HYHD.

Obv. As 139, but with different style of script

163. Æ ↑ 1.92. *Obv.* inscription as given in heading = YHW / ḤNNHKHN / HGDLW / ḤḆRH / YDM.
164. Æ ↘ 1.51. *Obv.* inscription in crude style, and incomplete: [YH]WḤN / HNḆ / WḤH / ḆR.

Obv. As 139, but with different style of script and change of text

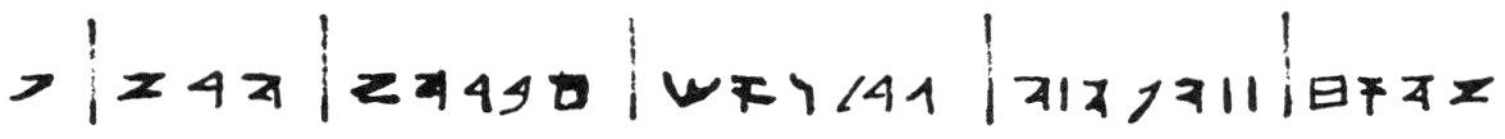

(Yehoḥanan the High Priest, Head of the Council of the Jews).

165. Æ ↑ 2.57. *Obv.* inscription as given in heading = YHWḤ / NNHKHNH / GDLR'Š / ḤḆRHY / HDY / M. *Rev.* to r., Greek letter Δ.
166. Æ ↑ 2.05. *Obv.* YHW / ḤNNHKHN / HGDLR' / ŠḤḆRH / YHDM.
167. Æ ↑ 2.37. *Obv.* YHW / ḤNNHKHN / HGDLR' [Š] / ḤḆRHY / HDY. *Rev.* to r., Greek letter Λ.
168. Æ ↑ 1.62. *Obv.* YHWNN[*sic*] / HKHNHG / DLR·ŠH / ḤḆRHY / HDY. *Rev.* to r., Greek letter Α.
169. Æ ↙ 1.76. *Obv.* YHWḤ / NNHKHN / HGDLR' / ŠHḤḆR / HYHD. *Rev.* as 165.

Obv. Inscription as 165, but incompletely preserved: ...KHNH / ŠHḤḆ.... Palm branch.
Rev. Lily flower.
Half prutah.

170. Æ ↗ 1.05. Cahn 71, 14 Oct. 1931, 587.

Obv. As 139, but with different style of script, and inscription often incomplete

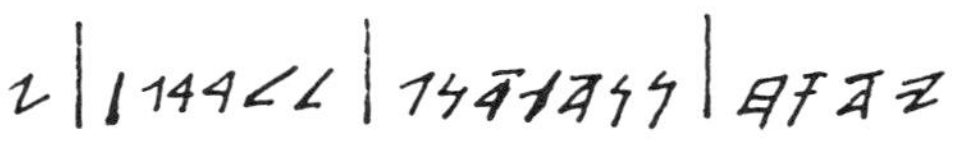

Rev. Double cornucopiae; in center, pomegranate.

171. Æ ↑ 2.15. *Obv.* inscription as given in heading = YHWḤ / NNHKHNG / LLDDGL / Y. *INS* 1.
172. Æ ↗ 2.22. *Obv.* YHWḤ / NNHKHN / HNLḤḆR / YHWD.
173. Æ ↑ 1.93. *Obv.* YHWḤ / NNKHN / GLDDL / Y.
174. Æ ↑ 2.01. *Obv.* YHWḤ / NNHKHN / GDLW.
175. Æ ↑ 2.20. *Obv.* YHWḤ / NNHKHN....

Obv. As 139, but with different style of script

176. Æ ↗ 1.45. *Obv.* inscription as given in heading = YH / ḤNNHKH / NHGDWL / ḤḆR....
177. Æ ↑ 2.23. *Obv.* YHW / ḤNNHK / HNWL / W.

JEWISH COINS: HASMONAEAN

John Hyrcanus II, Jerusalem (cont.)

178. Æ ↗ 2.12. *Obv.* YHW / ḤNNHK / HNLḤ / Y.
179. Æ ↑ 2.21. *Obv.* YHW / [Ḥ]NNHK / HNHGD / WḤ.
180. Æ ↑ 1.53. *Obv.* YHW / ḤNNHK / HNHGD / WḤB̄R.
181. Æ ↗ 1.37. *Obv.* YHW / ḤNNHK / HNH[/ WḤB̄R.
182. Æ ↑ 1.58. *Obv.* YHW / ḤNNH / KHNGD / LḤ̄.

Mattathias Antigonus (40–37 B.C.)
Mint of Jerusalem

Obv. Palaeo-Hebrew inscription

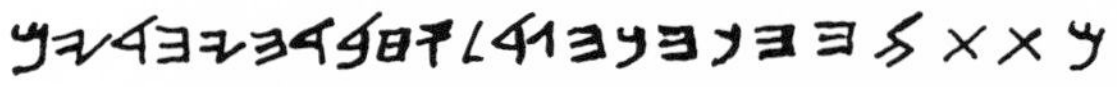

= MTTYHHKHNHGDLWḤB̄RHYHDYM (Mattitia the High Priest and the Council of the Jews) around and between double cornucopiae.
Rev. BACIΛΕΩC ANTIΓONOY around wreath.

183. Æ ↑ 14.27. *Obv.* MTTYH[HKHN]HGDLḤB̄RHY[HDYM]. *Rev.* [BA]CIΛЄƱC ANTI[ΓONOY]. *INS* 5.
184. Æ ↑ 15.01. *Obv.* MTTYHHKHNGDLḤB̄RHYH. *Rev.* BACIΛЄO ANT...
185. Æ ↖ 15.03. *Obv.* MTT...HGD...B̄RHYHD. *Rev.*]ΩC ANTI-ΓONOY.
186. Æ ↓ 14.61. *Obv.* ...TTY...B̄RYHDYM. *Rev.* ...AC...]ΩC.
187. Æ ↑ 13.88. Inscriptions illegible.
188. Æ ↘ 12.86. As 187.

Obv. As 183, but single cornucopiae.
Rev. As 183, but inscription is within wreath.

189. Æ ↑ 7.73. *Obv.* inscription only [M]TTYHKHN (Mattitia Priest). *Rev.* BACI ANT.
190. Æ ↙ 7.63. *Obv.*...HGDLḤ... ([Mattitia] the High [Priest] C[ouncil). *Rev.* BACIΛ ...ΩCA ....

Obv. Shortened Palaeo-Hebrew inscription as on 183: MTT / YH (Mattitia) within wreath.
Rev. Double cornucopiae; in center, pomegranate.

191. Æ → 1.60.

Obv. As 191, but inscription retrograde.
Rev. Double cornucopiae; in center, ear of grain.

192. Æ ↖ 1.92.
193. Æ ↓ 1.75.
194. Æ ↘ 1.67.

HERODIAN

On all coins of the Herodian Dynasty, obv. and rev. types are enclosed within a circular dotted border.

Herod the Great (40/37–4 B.C.)
Mint of Jerusalem

Obv. HΡΩΔΟΥ ΒΑΣΙΛΕΩΣ Tripod with lebes; to r., ⳨; to l., LΓ (37 B.C.).
Rev. Uncertain ceremonial object (apex?) flanked by two palm branches.

195. Æ ↑ 5.51. *INS* 6.
196. Æ ↑ 5.80.
197. Æ ↗ 7.65.
198. Æ ↗ 6.37.
199. Æ ↗ 5.98.
200. Æ ↗ 7.86.

Obv. HΡΩΔΟΥ ΒΑΣΙΛΕΩΣ Crested helmet; to r., ⳨; to l., LΓ (37 B.C.).
Rev. Decorated shield.

201. Æ ↑ 3.83.

Obv. HΡΩΔΟΥ ΒΑΣΙΛΕΩΣ Winged caduceus; to r., ⳨; to l., LΓ (37 B.C.).
Rev. Poppy head.

202. Æ ↗ 3.09.

Obv. HPƱ∇OY BACIΛEΩC [*sic*] X within diadem.
Rev. Table flanked by two palm branches.

203. Æ ↓ 3.64.
204. Æ ↑ 3.43.
205. Æ ↓ 3.35.

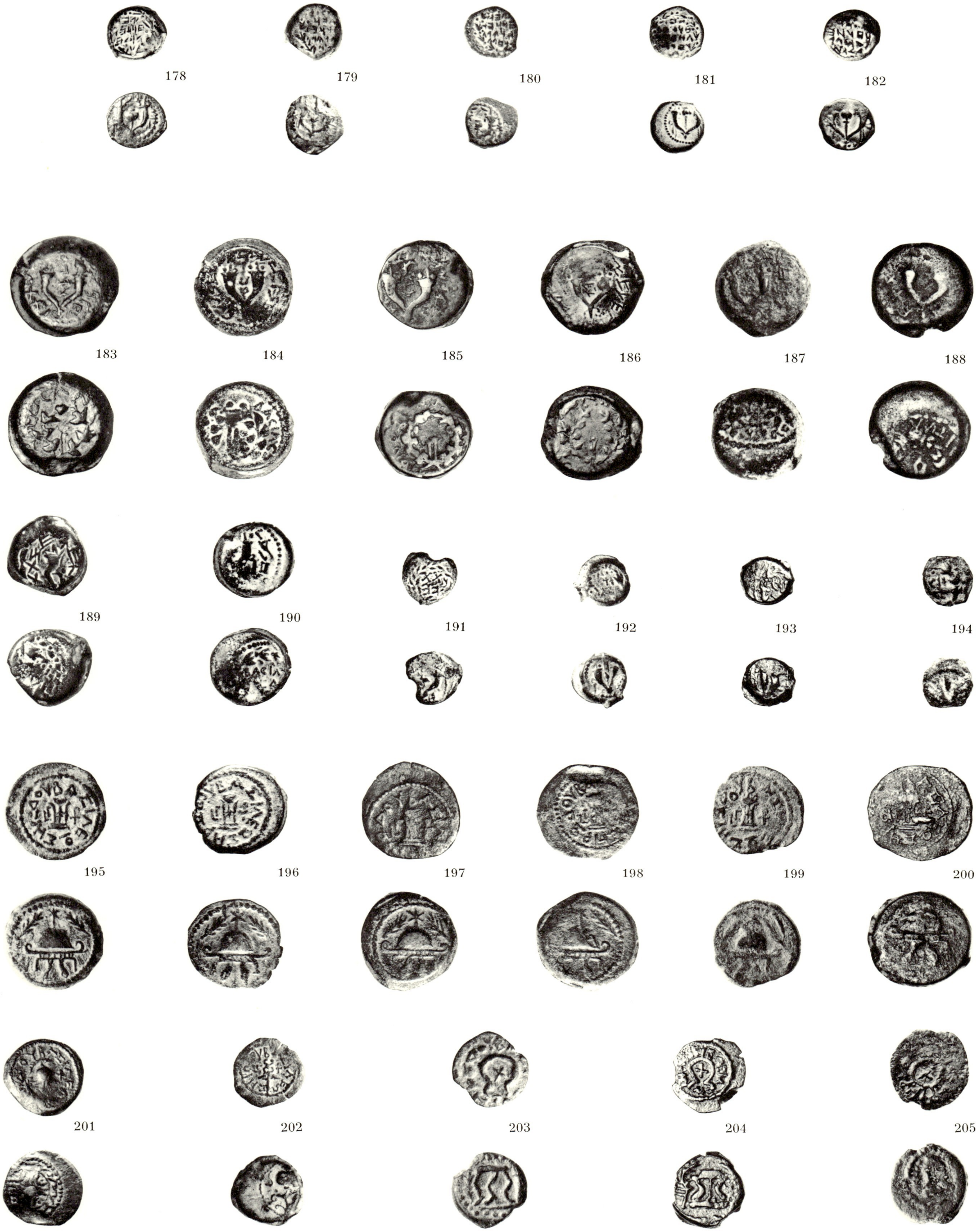

178 179 180 181 182

183 184 185 186 187 188

189 190 191 192 193 194

195 196 197 198 199 200

201 202 203 204 205

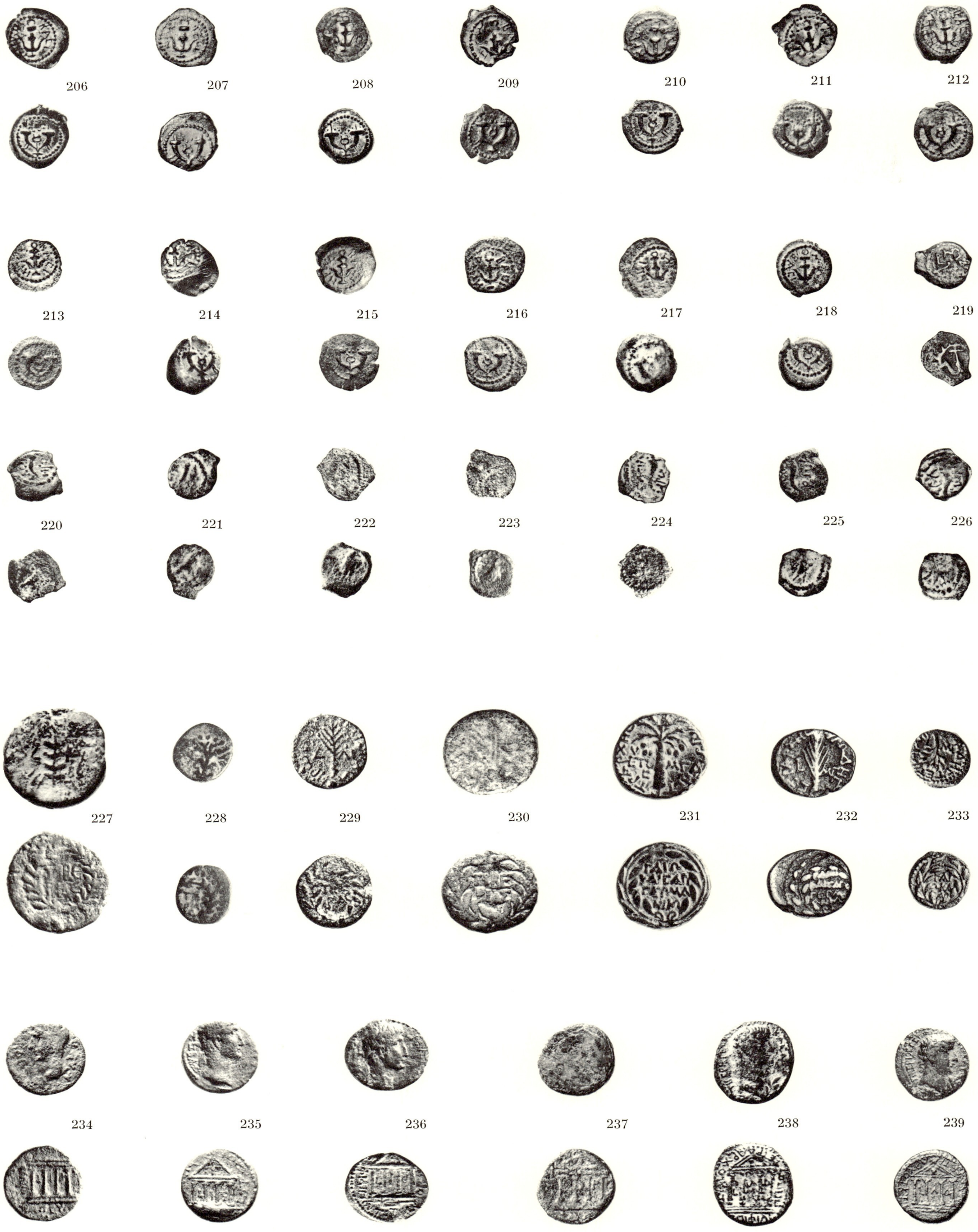
206 207 208 209 210 211 212
213 214 215 216 217 218 219
220 221 222 223 224 225 226
227 228 229 230 231 232 233
234 235 236 237 238 239

JEWISH COINS: HERODIAN

Herod the Great, Jerusalem (cont.)

> *Obv.*   HPω / BACI   Anchor.
> *Rev.*   Double cornucopiae with caduceus between the horns.

206. Æ ↗ 1.65.
207. Æ ↙ 1.54.
208. Æ → 2.02.
209. Æ ↗ 1.34.
210. Æ ↗ 1.53.
211. Æ ↑ 1.97.
212. Æ ↓ 1.87.
213. Æ ↖ 0.96.
214. Æ ↖ 1.70.
215. Æ ↑ 1.74.
216. Æ ↓ 1.65. *Obv.* HPωΔ / BACI
217. Æ ↑ 1.60. *Obv.* BACI / HPω
218. Æ ↖ 1.77. *Obv.* BACI / HPω (outward).

> *Obv.*   BACIΛE / HPω
> *Rev.*   Anchor surrounded by a wheel with horizontal lines.

219. Æ ↙ ? 0.80.

> *Obv.*   BACI / HPωΔ   Single cornucopiae.
> *Rev.*   Eagle standing r.

220. Æ ↓ 1.07.
221. Æ ↓ 0.84.
222. Æ ↓ 0.92.
223. Æ ↓ 0.90.
224. Æ ↑ 0.97.
225. Æ ← 0.86.
226. Æ ↑ 0.90.

Herod Antipas (4 B.C.–A.D. 39)
Mint of Tiberias

> *Obv.*   HPωΔOY TETPAPXOY (227–29, sometimes incompletely preserved), HPΩΔHC TETPAP XHC (231–33), or illegible inscription (230); reed (227–28), palm branch (229–30, 232), palm tree (231) or bunch of date fruits (233).
> *Rev.*   TIBE/PIAC (227–30), ΓAIΩ KAICAP / ΓEPMA / NIK (231), ΓAIω / KAICAP / ΓEPM / ANI (232), or ΓAI / ΩKA / CAP (233), within wreath.

227. Æ ↘ 17.14. *Obv.* to l. and r., L KΔ (A.D. 19/20).
228. Æ ↘ 2.68. *Obv.* date as 227.
229. Æ ↑ 4.92. *Obv.* to l., and r. LΛΓ (A.D. 28/9).
230. Æ ↑ 11.96. *Obv.* date illegible.
231. Æ ↗ 12.58. *Obv.* ETO / C / MΓ (A.D. 38/9).
232. Æ ↑ 7.05. *Obv.* to l. and r., L MΓ (A.D. 38/9).
233. Æ ↑ 3.55. *Obv.* date as 232.

Herod Philippus (4 B.C.–A.D. 34)
Mint of Caesarea Panias

> *Obv.*   KAICAPCEBACTOC (234–35) or TIBEPIOCCE BACKAICAP (236–39, sometimes incompletely preserved); head of Augustus l. (234) or r. (235), or laureate head of Tiberius r. (236, 238–39), or inscription and type illegible (237).
> *Rev.*   ΦIΛIΠΠOY TETPAPXOY (234–37, sometimes incompletely preserved), or EΠIΦIΛIΠΠOY TETPAPXOY KTI (238–39, incompletely preserved on 239). Tetrastyle temple (the Augusteum in Panias). In between columns, date.

234. Æ ↑ 4.85. *Rev.* LIB (A.D. 9).
235. Æ ↑ 7.34. LIϚ (A.D. 13).
236. Æ ↑ 4.82. LIΘ (A.D. 16).
237. Æ ↑ 6.02. LΛΓ (A.D. 30).
238. Æ ↑ 6.21. *Obv.* to r., laurel branch. *Rev.* LΛΔ (A.D. 31). Note the additional epithet, *ktistes*, founder. *INS* 9.
239. Æ ↑ 5.82. As 238.

JEWISH COINS: HERODIAN (cont.)

Herod Archelaus (4 B.C.–A.D. 6)
Mint of Jerusalem

Obv. Parallel double cornucopiae.
Rev. Galley l., with aphlaston and oars.

240. Æ ↑ 2.22. *Obv.* ΗΡ.... *Rev.* ЄΘΝΑ / ΡΧ / ΗC.
241. Æ ↖ 1.48. *Obv.* ΗΡѠΔ. *Rev.* ЄΘΝ / Α. Half unit of 240.
242. Æ ↖ 0.98. As 241.

Obv. Η / Ρ / Ѡ Prow of galley l.
Rev. ЄΘΝ within wreath.

243. Æ ↑ 1.06.
244. Æ ↗ 1.35.
245. Æ ↑ 1.31.
246. Æ ↑ 1.19.
247. Æ → 1.46.
248. Æ ↓ 1.44.
249. Æ ↗ 0.92.
250. Æ ↑ 1.33.

Obv. ΗΡѠ / Δ / ΟΥ (sometimes incompletely preserved). Anchor.
Rev. ЄΘ / ΡΑΝ / ΥΟΧ (sometimes abbreviated) within wreath.

251. Æ ↓ 0.81.
252. Æ ↘ 1.48.
253. Æ ↑ 0.57.
254. Æ ↑ 0.99.

Obv. ΗΡѠΔΟΥ Bunch of grapes.
Rev. ЄΘΝΑΡΧ Crested helmet; to l., downward, small caduceus.

255. Æ ↓ 2.20. *INS* 7.
256. Æ ↓ 2.03.
257. Æ ↓ 2.18.
258. Æ ↓ 2.00.
259. Æ ↑ 2.45.
260. Æ → 2.01.

Agrippa I (A.D. 37–44)
Mint of Tiberias

Obv. ΣΕΒΑΣΤΩ Head of Caligula l.
Rev. ΝΟ ... / ΒΑΣΙΛ ... / ΑΓΡΙΠΠΑ Agrippa standing r. in quadriga, holding scepter.

261. Æ ↑ 11.64.

Mint of Jerusalem

Obv. ΒΑCΙΛΕѠC ΑΓΡΙΠΑ Canopy.
Rev. Three ears of grain; to l. and r., LϚ (A.D. 42).

262. Æ ↑ 2.11.
263. Æ ↑ 2.84.
264. Æ ↑ 3.18.
265. Æ ↑ 3.62.
266. Æ ↑ 2.29.
267. Æ ↑ 2.61.
268. Æ ↑ 3.07.
269. Æ ↑ 2.65.
270. Æ ↑ 2.21.
271. Æ ↑ 2.31. *INS* 10.
272. Æ ↑ 1.69. Doublestruck.
273. Æ ↑ 2.79. Brockage.

Mint of Caesarea

Obv. ...ϹΑΡΒΑϹ .... Laureate head of Agrippa r.; countermark on neck: head.
Rev. ΚΑΙϹΑΡΙΑ Η Π .... Tyche of Caesarea standing l., holding rudder and palm branch; to r., LΗ (A.D. 41).

274. Æ ↑ 9.06.

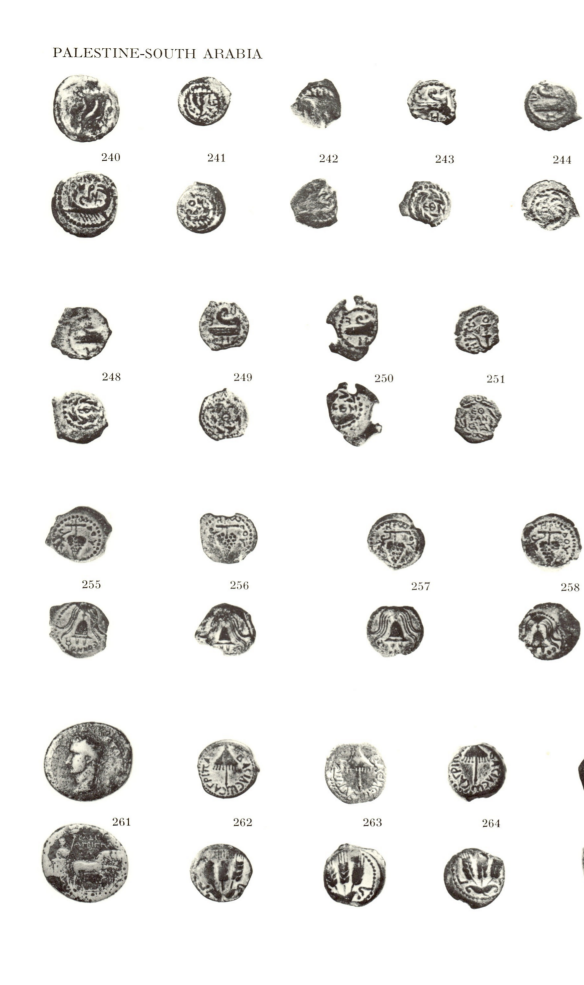

240 241 242 243 244 245 246 247

248 249 250 251 252 253 254

255 256 257 258 259 260

261 262 263 264 265 266 267

268 269 270 271 272 273 274

275 276 277 278 279 280 281 282

283 284 285 286 287 288

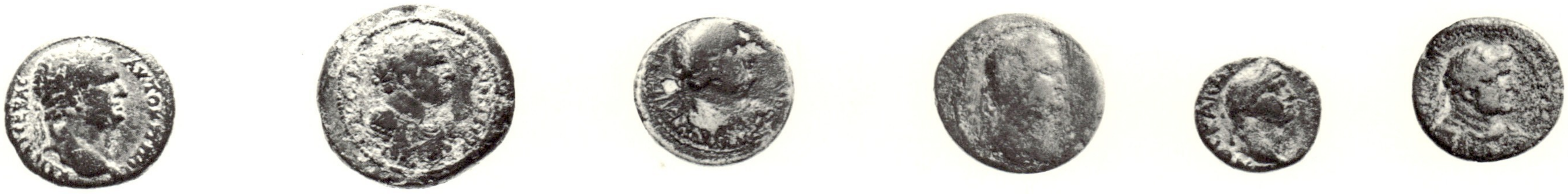

289 290 291 292 293 294

295 296 297 298 299 300 301 302

JEWISH COINS: HERODIAN (cont.)

Agrippa II (ca. A.D. 50–95)

Probably mint of Caesarea Panias.

The Classical era used by Agrippa II began in A.D. 56. Nevertheless, most of his coins are dated according to the era of 61, marking the refounding of Caesarea Panias as Neronias. See Y. Meshorer, *Jewish Coins of the Second Temple Period* (Tel Aviv, 1967), pp. 81–87.

(Under Nero)

Obv. ...ΣΕΒΑΣΤΟΣ.... Radiate head of Nero r.
Rev. ΕΠΙ / ΒΑCΙΛΕ / ΑΓΡΙΠΠ / ΝΕΡΩ / ΝΙΕ within wreath (A.D. 61).

275. Æ ↑ 12.62. *Obv.* to r., small lituus.
276. Æ ↑ 13.35. *Obv.* as 275.
277. Æ ↑ 12.37. *Obv.* as 275. Countermark on neck: uncertain.
278. Æ ↑ 6.49. Half unit of 275.
279. Æ ↑ 3.26. Quarter unit of 275.
280. Æ ↑ 3.26. Quarter unit of 275.
281. Æ ↑ 3.42. Quarter unit of 275.

Obv. ΒΑCΙΛΕΩC ΜΑΡΚΟΥ ΑΓΡΙΠΠΟΥ Hand holding ears of corn and small unidentified fruit.
Rev. ΕΤΟΥC ΑΙΤΟΥ In center, ⩪, representing the numeral ϛ (6) and Κ (ΚΑΙ); dated according to the two eras of Agrippa II, year 11 which is also year 6 (A.D. 66/7).

282. Æ ↑ 1.55.

(Under Vespasian)

Obv. Laureate head of Vespasian r.
Rev. ΒΑ/[Α]ΓΡΙΠΠΑ (sometimes incompletely preserved). Tyche standing l., holding ears of corn and cornucopiae.

283. Æ ↑ 16.94. *Obv.* ΚΑΙCΑΡCΕΒΑCΤΩ.... *Rev.* ΕΤΟΥ ΚϚ (A.D. 86/7).
284. Æ ↑ 18.21. *Obv.* ΑΥΤΟΚΡΑΟΥΕCΠ ... CΑΡCΕΒΑCΤω. *Rev.* in upper l., small star; [Ε]ΤΟΥ ΚΖ (A.D. 87/8).
285. Æ ↑ 13.04. *Obv.* ΑVΤΟΚΡΑΟΥΕ... ΑΝΩ ΚΑΙCΑΡΙCΕ-ΒΑCΤΩ *Rev.* ΤΟΥ ΚΘ (A.D. 89/90).

(Under Titus)

Obv. ΑΥΤΟΚΡΤΙΤΟC ΚΑΙCΑΡCΕΒ (sometimes abbreviated or incompletely preserved). Bust of Titus r., laureate (286–89) or laureate and draped (290–92).
Rev. ΒΑ ΑΓΡΙΠΠΑ Nike advancing r., holding wreath and palm branch (286, 289–92), Tyche standing l., holding ears of corn and cornucopiae (287), or galley sailing l. (288).

286. Æ ↑ 9.57. *Rev.* ΒΑC ΑΓΡΙΠΠΟΥ LΙΔ (A.D. 74/5).
287. Æ ↖ 15.65. *Rev.* ΕΤΟ ΙΘ (A.D. 79/80).
288. Æ ↖ 7.91. *Rev.* date as 287.
289. Æ ↑ 11.64. *Rev.* ΕΤΟ ΚϚ (A.D. 86/7).
290. Æ ↑ 15.08. *Rev.* date as 289.
291. Æ ↑ 13.88. *Rev.* ΤΟ ΚΘ (A.D. 89/90).
292. Æ ↑ 11.79. *Rev.* date as 291.

(Under Domitian)

Obv. ΔΟΜΕΤΙΑΝΟCΚΑΙCΑΡ (293, 305, 307–13, sometimes abbreviated or incompletely preserved), ΔΟΜΕΤΚΑΙCΑΡΓΕΡΜ (294–304, sometimes abbreviated or incompletely preserved), ΔΟ-ΜΙΤΙΑΝΟC ΚΑΙCΑΡ (314), or ΚΔΟΜΙΤΑΚΑΙ-CΑΡΑΓΕΡ (315) Bust of Domitian r., laureate (293, 296–317), or laureate and draped (294–5).
Rev. ΒΑ ΑΓΡΙΠΠΑ (sometimes abbreviated or incompletely preserved). Nike standing l. (293) or r. (298–303, 305, 307–12, 314), writing on a shield that rests on raised knee; Nike advancing r., holding wreath and palm branch (294–95); inscription within wreath (296–97, 316–17); one cornucopiae (304); double cornucopiae (313); Moneta standing l., holding scales and cornucopiae (306); or Tyche standing l., holding ears of corn and cornucopiae (315).

293. Æ ↑ 5.67. *Rev.* LΙΔ (A.D. 74/5).
294. Æ ↑ 9.58. *Rev.* ΕΤΟ ΚΔ (A.D. 84/5).
295. Æ ↑ 10.32. *Rev.* date as 294.
296. Æ ↑ 5.96. *Rev.* date as 294.
297. Æ ↑ 5.85. *Rev.* date as 294.
298. Æ ↑ 4.88. *Rev.* in lower l., crescent. Date as 294.
299. Æ ↑ 4.61. *Rev.* as 298.
300. Æ ↑ 5.09. *Rev.* as 298.
301. Æ ↑ 5.24. *Rev.* as 298. *INS* 11.
302. Æ ↑ 4.34. *Rev.* as 298.

JEWISH COINS: HERODIAN

Agrippa II (under Domitian), Caesarea Panias (cont.)

303. Æ → 4.43. *Obv.* countermark: emperor's (Trajan's?) head. *Rev.* as 298.
304. Æ ↑ 1.71. *Rev.* ET KE (A.D. 85/6).
305. Æ ↖ 6.72. *Rev.* in upper r., small crescent. ETO KϚ (A.D. 86/7).
306. Æ ↓ 8.61. Doublestruck. *Obv.* [DIVIVES] PFDOMITIAN AVG-GERCO [SXII] *Rev.* MONETA EΠIBA[AΓPAVG]VSTI / ETKϚ SC (A.D. 86/7). For the attribution to Caesarea Panias, see Y. Meshorer, "A New Type of Coins of Agrippa II," *IEJ* 21 (1971), pp. 164–65.
307. Æ ↑ 6.49. *Rev.* in upper r., small star. Date as 305.
308. Æ ↑ 5.24. *Rev.* date as 305.
309. Æ ↑ 3.82. *Obv.* two countermarks (head of emperor?). *Rev.* date as 305.
310. Æ ↑ 6.34. *Obv.* countermark: as 309. *Rev.* date as 305.
311. Æ ↑ 7.07. *Obv.* countermark: X̄ (Tenth Roman Legion). *Rev.* date as 305.
312. Æ ↑ 4.50. *Rev.* ETO KZ (A.D. 87/8).
313. Æ ↑ 3.92. *Rev.* date as 312.
314. Æ ↑ 6.90. *Rev.* E⊥OΛ KΘ (A.D. 89/90).
315. Æ ↑ 17.42. $\overline{\text{E}}$TOV $\overline{\text{EΛ}}$ (A.D. 95/6).
316. Æ ↓ 3.11. *Rev.* date as 315.
317. Æ ↓ 2.29. *Rev.* date as 315.

Obv. BAAΓP Bust of Tyche r.
Rev. Single cornucopiae. $\overline{\text{E}}$T $\overline{\text{Δ}}$Λ (A.D. 94/5).

318. Æ ↑ 2.39.
319. Æ ↑ 1.86.
320. Æ ↑ 1.72.

JEWISH COINS: ROMAN PROCURATORS

On all coins of the Roman Procurators, obv. and rev. types are enclosed within a circular dotted border.

(Under Augustus)
Coponius (A.D. 6–9)

Obv. KAICAPOC Ear of grain.
Rev. Palm tree; to l. and r., L ΛϚ (A.D. 6).

321. Æ ↑ 2.14.
322. Æ ↑ 2.05.
323. Æ ↑ 1.85.
324. Æ ↓ 1.70.
325. Æ ↑ 1.35.

Ambibulus (A.D. 9–12)

Obv. KAICAPOC Ear of grain.
Rev. Palm tree.

326. Æ ↑ 2.24. *Rev.* to l. and r., L ΛΘ (A.D. 9).
327. Æ ↑ 2.81. *Rev.* as 326.
328. Æ ↑ 2.44. *Rev.* as 326.
329. Æ ↑ 2.16. *Rev.* as 326.
330. Æ ↓ 2.35. *Rev.* as 326.
331. Æ ↑ 2.12. *Rev.* to l. and r., L M (A.D. 10).
332. Æ ↓ 2.73. *Rev.* as 331.
333. Æ ↑ 1.96. *Rev.* to l. and r., L MA (A.D. 11).
334. Æ ↑ 1.76. *Rev.* as 333.
335. Æ ↑ 1.57. *Rev.* as 333.
336. Æ ↖ 1.88. *Rev.* as 333.

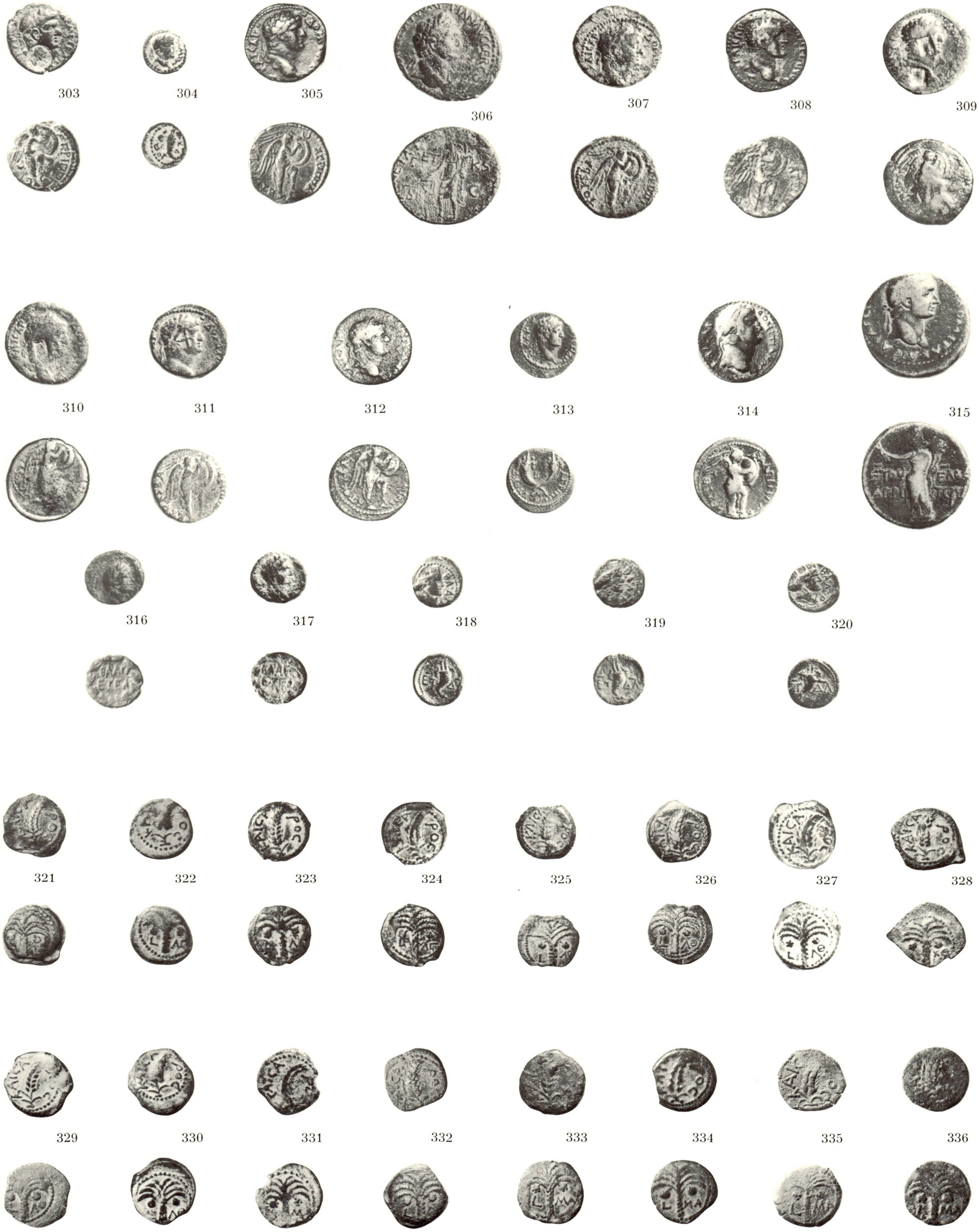

303 304 305 306 307 308 309

310 311 312 313 314 315

316 317 318 319 320

321 322 323 324 325 326 327 328

329 330 331 332 333 334 335 336

337 338 339 340 341 342 343 344

345 346 347 348 349 350 351 352

353 354 355 356 357 358 359 360

361 362 363 364 365 366 367 368

369 370 371 372 373 374 375 376

JEWISH COINS: ROMAN PROCURATORS

Ambibulus (cont.)

337. Æ ↖ 1.76. *Rev.* as 333.
338. Æ ↑ 1.89. *Rev.* as 333.

(Under Tiberius)
Valerius Gratus (A.D. 15–26)

Obv. KAI CAP within wreath.
Rev. TIB Double cornucopiae with LB (A.D. 15) between the horns.

339. Æ ↖ 1.45.

Obv. IOY ΛIA within wreath,
Rev. Laurel branch; to l. and r., L B (A.D. 15).

340. Æ ↓ 1.95.

Obv. As 339.
Rev. TIBЄIPOY [*sic*]. Double cornucopiae with caduceus between the horns; to l. and r., L Γ (A.D. 16).

341. Æ ↘ 1.87.
342. Æ ↓ 1.55.
343. Æ ↓ 1.30. *Rev.* TIBЄPIOY.

Obv. As 340.
Rev. Three lilies; to l. and r., L Γ (A.D. 16).

344. Æ ↘ 1.79.
345. Æ ↑ 2.51.
346. Æ ↓ 1.59.
347. Æ ↑ 1.73.

Obv. IOVΛIA Vine branch with leaf, small bunch of grapes and tendril.
Rev. Amphora; to l. and r., L Δ (A.D. 17).

348. Æ ↓ 1.63.
349. Æ ↓ 1.82.
350. Æ ↙ 1.48.

Obv. TIBEPIOV Vine branch with leaf and tendril.
Rev. Cantharus; to l. and r., L Δ (A.D. 17).

351. Æ ↓ 1.63.
352. Æ ↑ 1.77.

Obv. TIB KAI CAP within wreath.
Rev. IOVΛIA Palm branch.

353. Æ ↑ 2.27. *Rev.* to l. and r., Λ Δ (A.D. 17).
354. Æ ↑ 2.36. *Rev.* as 353.
355. Æ ↑ 2.07. *Rev.* as 353.
356. Æ → 2.25. *Rev.* to l. and r., L Є (A.D. 18).
357. Æ ↓ 2.33. *Rev.* as 356.
358. Æ ↑ 2.01. *Rev.* as 356.
359. Æ ↘ 2.38. *Rev.* as 356.
360. Æ ↑ 1.87. *Rev.* as 356.
361. Æ → 2.46. *Rev.* as 356.
362. Æ ↑ 2.25. *Rev.* as 356.
363. Æ ↑ 2.41. *Rev.* to l. and r., L IA (A.D. 24).
364. Æ ↑ 1.85. *Rev.* as 363.
365. Æ ↖ 2.27. *Rev.* as 363.
366. Æ ↓ 1.98. *Rev.* as 363.

Pontius Pilatus (A.D. 26–36)

Obv. TIBEPIOV KAICAPOC LIϚ (A.D. 29). Simpulum.
Rev. IOVΛIA KAICAPOC Three ears of grain.

367. Æ ↑ 2.31.
368. Æ ↖ 2.53.
369. Æ ↖ 1.90.
370. Æ ↑ 2.29.
371. Æ ↑ 2.03.
372. Æ ↑ 2.67.

Obv. TIBEPIOV KAICAPOC Lituus.
Rev. Date within wreath.

373. Æ ↑ 2.01. *Rev.* LIZ (A.D. 30).
374. Æ ↑ 2.57. *Rev.* as 373.
375. Æ ↑ 2.28. *Rev.* as 373.
376. Æ ↑ 1.97. *Rev.* as 373.

JEWISH COINS: ROMAN PROCURATORS

Pontius Pilatus (cont.)

377. Æ ↑ 1.89. *Rev.* as 373.
378. Æ ↖ 2.59. *Rev.* as 373.
379. Æ ↑? 1.22. *Rev.* brockage.
380. Æ ↑ 1.62. *Rev.* LIꟻ = LIZ (A.D. 30).
381 Æ ↘ 2.15. *Rev.* as 380.
382. Æ ↖ 1.86. *Rev.* as 380.
383. Æ ↖ 1.88. *Rev.* HZ = LIZ (A.D. 30)
384. Æ ↑ 1.56. *Rev.* as 383.
385. Æ ↑ 1.73. *Rev.* LIH (A.D. 31).
386. Æ ↖ 2.22. *Rev.* as 385.
387. Æ ↑ 2.00. *Rev.* as 385 but date retrograde.

(Under Claudius)
Antonius Felix (A.D. 52–59)

Obv. IOV / ΛΙΑΑΓ / ΡΙΠΠΙ / ΝΑ Within wreath.
Rev. ΤΙΚΛΑVΔΙΟϹΚΑΙϹΑΡ ΓΕΡΜ Two palm branches crossed; below, LIΔ (A.D. 54).

388. Æ ↖ 2.52.
389. Æ ↑ 2.39.
390. Æ ↑ 2.46.
391. Æ ↑ 2.44.
392. Æ ↑ 2.89.
393. Æ ↖ 2.26.
394. Æ ↑ 2.96.
395. Æ ↓ 2.14. *Rev.* inscription retrograde.
396. Æ ↑? 2.58.

Obv. ΝΕΡΩΚΛΑVΚΑΙϹΑΡ Two shields and two spears crossed.
Rev. ΒΡΙΤ / ΚΑΙ Palm tree; to l. and r., L IΔ (A.D. 54).

397. Æ ↗ 2.79.
398. Æ ↗ 2.78.
399. Æ ↓ 3.06.
400. Æ ↘ 2.85.
401. Æ ← 2.69.
402. Æ → 2.52.
403. Æ ↗ 2.49.
404. Æ ↖ 2.59.

(Under Nero)
Porcius Festus (A.D. 59–62)

Obv. ΝΕΡ / ΩΝΟ / C Within wreath.
Rev. LЄ ΚΑΙϹΑΡΟϹ Palm branch. (A.D. 59).

405. Æ ↓ 2.37.
406. Æ ↓ 3.63.
407. Æ ↑ 2.28.
408. Æ ↑ 1.84.
409. Æ ↑ 3.27.
410. Æ ↑ 2.37.
411. Æ ← 2.34. *Obv.* last letter, C, in inscription written ⌒.
412. Æ ↑ 2.22.
413. Æ ↑ 1.59.
414. Æ ↑ 1.72.
415. Æ ↑ 2.00. *Obv.* letters, N, retrograde.
416. Æ ↖ 1.49. *Rev.* inscription retrograde.
417. Æ ↑ 1.28. *Obv.* inscription retrograde.
418. Æ ↑ 2.04. Very crude style, inscriptions garbled.

377 378 379 380 381 382 383 384 385

386 387 388 389 390 391 392 393 394

395 396 397 398 399 400 401 402

403 404 405 406 407 408 409 410

411 412 413 414 415 416 417 418

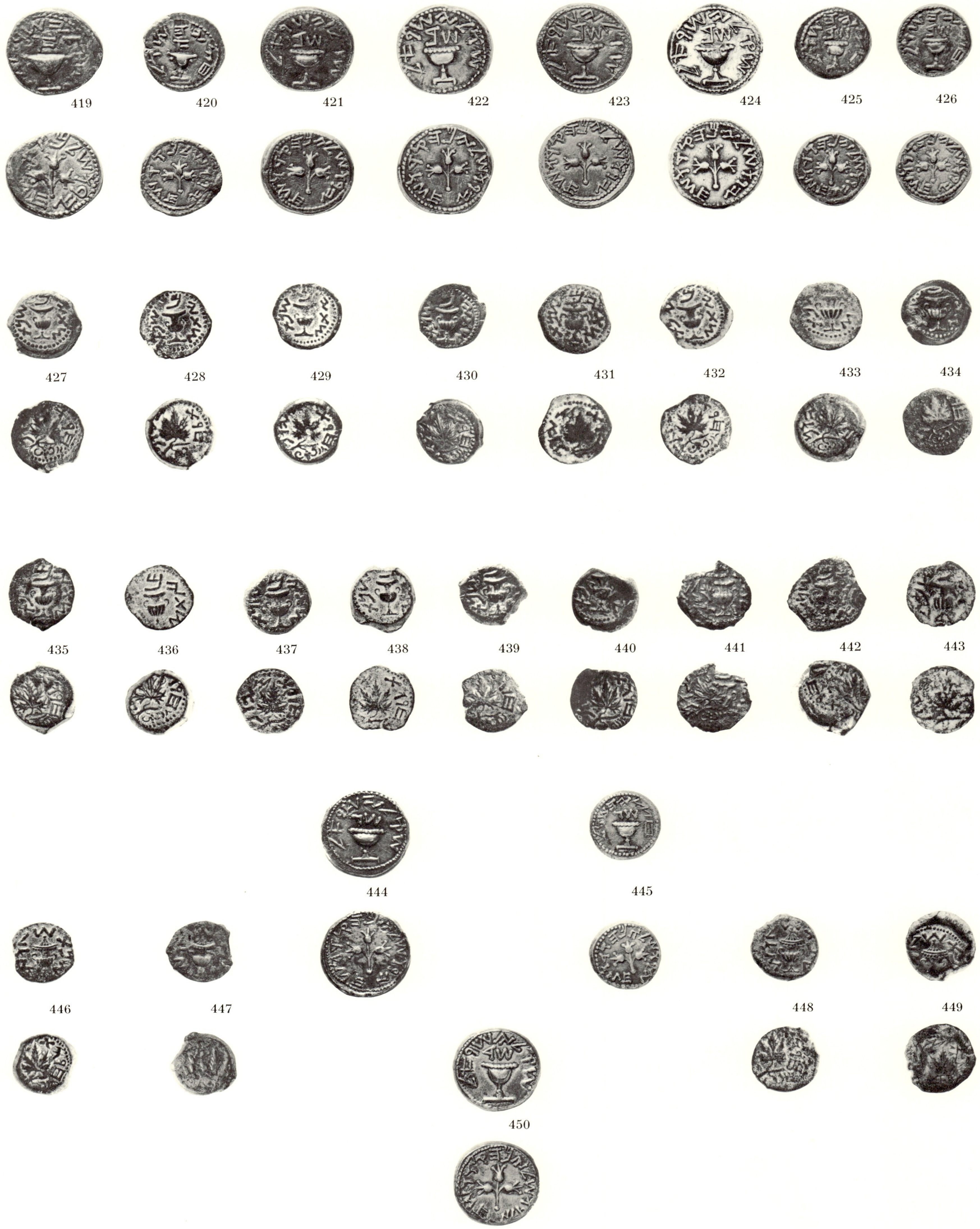

419 420 421 422 423 424 425 426

427 428 429 430 431 432 433 434

435 436 437 438 439 440 441 442 443

444 445

446 447 448 449

450

JEWISH COINS: JEWISH WAR AGAINST ROME

The vine leaf on nos. 427–43 and 446–49 has been turned upward so that the relative position to each other of the die axis and the inscription conforms to that of the other coins of this section. Obv. and rev. types are all enclosed within a circular dotted border.

Obv. Palaeo-Hebrew inscriptions 𐤔𐤒𐤋 𐤉𐤔𐤓𐤀𐤋 (419, 421–24), 𐤇𐤑𐤉 𐤄𐤔𐤒𐤋 (420, 425–26). Chalice.
Rev. Palaeo-Hebrew inscriptions 𐤉𐤓𐤅𐤔𐤋𐤌 𐤒𐤃𐤔𐤄 (419–20), 𐤉𐤓𐤅𐤔𐤋𐤉𐤌 𐤄𐤒𐤃𐤅𐤔𐤄 (421–26). Stem with three pomegranates.
Shekels (419, 421–24), half-shekels (420, 425–26).

419. AR ↑ 11.82. *Obv.* ŠQLYŚR'L (shekel of Israel); above chalice, Hebrew date 𐤀 = ʿ, year 1 (A.D. 66). *Rev.* YRWŠLMQDŠH (holy Jerusalem).
420. AR ↖ 6.75. *Obv.* ḤṢYHŠQL (half the shekel); date as 419. *Rev.* As 419.
421. AR ↑ 13.83. *Obv.* inscription as 419; above chalice, Hebrew date 𐤔𐤁 = ŠB, year 2 (A.D. 67). *Rev.* YRWŠLYMHQ-DWŠH (Jerusalem the holy).
422. AR ↑ 13.92. As 421.
423. AR ↑ 14.24. As 421.
424. AR ↑ 14.11. As 421.
425. AR ↑ 6.84. *Obv.* inscription as 420; date as 421. *Rev.* as 421.
426. AR ↑ 6.53. As 425.

Obv. Palaeo-Hebrew inscription 𐤔𐤍𐤕 𐤔𐤕𐤉𐤌 = ŠNTŠTYM, year 2 (A.D. 67). Amphora.
Rev. Palaeo-Hebrew inscription 𐤇𐤓𐤕 𐤑𐤉𐤅𐤍 = ḤRT ṢYWN (freedom of Zion). Vine leaf with tendril.

427. Æ ↓ 2.78.
428. Æ ↓ 3.59.
429. Æ ↓ 2.43.
430. Æ ↓ 2.56. *INS* 16.
431. Æ ↓ 2.79.
432. Æ ↓ 2.75.
433. Æ ↓ 3.48.
434. Æ ↘ 3.10.
435. Æ ↓ 2.57. *Rev.* variant, ḤRWT ṢYWN.
436. Æ ↓ 3.64.
437. Æ ↓ 3.13.
438. Æ ↓ 3.07.
439. Æ ↓ 2.97.
440. Æ ↓ 2.73.
441. Æ ↓ 2.28. Restruck.: both obv. and rev. types visible on each side of coin.
442. Æ ↓ 3.45. Doublestruck. *INS* 13.
443. Æ ↘ 1.60. Crude style.

Obv. Palaeo-Hebrew inscriptions as 419 (444), as 420 (445). Chalice; above, Hebrew date 𐤔𐤂 = ŠG, year 3 (A.D. 68).
Rev. Palaeo-Hebrew inscription as 421. Stem with three pomegranates.
Shekel (444), half shekel (445).

444. Æ ↑ 14.11. *INS* 14.
445. Æ ↑ 6.98.

Obv. Palaeo-Hebrew inscription 𐤔𐤍𐤕 𐤔𐤋𐤅𐤔 = ŠNT ŠLWŠ, year 3 (A.D. 68). Amphora with lid.
Rev. Palaeo-Hebrew inscription as 435. Vine leaf with tendril.

446. Æ ↓ 2.66.
447. Æ ↓ 2.81.
448. Æ ↓ 2.77. *INS* 17.
449. Æ ↓ 2.90.

Obv. Palaeo-Hebrew inscription as 419. Chalice; above, Hebrew date 𐤔𐤃 = ŠD, year 4 (A.D. 69).
Rev. Palaeo-Hebrew inscription as 421. Stem with three pomegranates.
Shekel.

450. Æ ↑ 14.17.

JEWISH COINS: JEWISH WAR AGAINST ROME (cont.)

Obv. Palaeo-Hebrew inscription
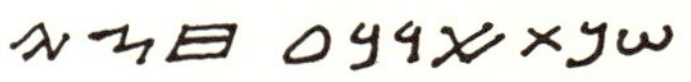 = ŠNT ’RB‘ḤṢY, year 4, half (A.D. 69). Ethrog (citron) between two lulavs (composed of palm branch, myrtle and willow).
Rev. Palaeo-Hebrew inscription
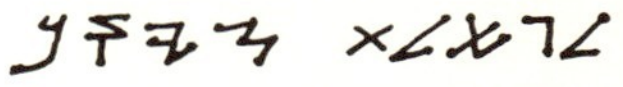 = LG’ LT ṢYWN (for the redemption of Zion). Palm tree; to l. and r., two baskets of dates. No. 451 is apparently an emergency bronze half shekel.

451. Æ ↑ 14.87.

Obv. Palaeo-Hebrew inscription
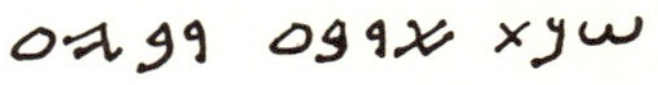 = ŠNT ’RB‘RB̲Y‘ year 4, quarter (A.D. 69). Two lulavs (the species of Tabernacles).
Rev. Inscription as 450. Ethrog.

Nos. 452–54 are apparently emergency bronze quarter shekels.

452. Æ ↑ 9.76.
453. Æ ↑ 9.71.
454. Æ ↑ 8.36.

Obv. Palaeo-Hebrew inscription  = ŠNT ’RB‘, year 4 (A.D. 69). Lulav between two ethrogs.
Rev. Inscription as 451. Chalice.

455. Æ ↑ 6.29.
456. Æ ↑ 5.76.
457. Æ ↑ 5.45.
458. Æ ↑ 5.86.
459. Æ ↖ 4.73.
460. Æ ↑ 4.46.
461. Æ ↑ 4.57. *INS* 15.

JEWISH COINS: JUDAEA CAPTA

On all coins of Judaea Capta, obv. and rev. types are enclosed within a circular dotted border.

Vespasian (A.D. 69–79)
Mint of Caesarea

Obv. ΑΥΤΟΚΡΟΥ ΕΣΠΚΑΙΣΣΕΒ Laureate head of Vespasian r.
Rev. ΙΟΥΔΑΙΑΣ ΕΑΛΩΚΥΙΑΣ Nike standing r., resting foot on helmet, writing on shield hung from palm tree.

462. Æ ↑ 7.85.
463. Æ ↑ 7.83. *Obv.* countermark: head (emperor?); *Rev.* countermark: galley (emblem of the Tenth Roman Legion).

Titus (A.D. 79–81)
Mint of Caesarea

Obv. ΑVΤΟΚΡΤΙΤΟ ΣΚΑΙΣΑΡ Laureate head of Titus r.
Rev. ΙΟVΔΑΙΑϹΕΑ ΛѠΚVΙΑϹ Nike standing r., resting foot on helmet, writing on shield hung from palm tree.

464. Æ ↑ 8.30.
465. Æ ↑ 8.52.
466. Æ ↑ 6.14.
467. Æ ↑ 8.88.
468. Æ ↑ 6.28. *Rev.* countermark: ΚΑΙ.
469. Æ ↑ 8.14.
470. Æ ↑ 7.14.
471. Æ ↑ 7.35.
472. Æ ↑ 6.88. *Obv.* countermark: head (emperor?); *Rev.* countermark as 463.
473. Æ ↑ 6.86. *Obv.* and *rev.* countermarks as 472.
474. Æ ↑ 6.31. *Rev.* ΙΟΥΔΑΙΑΣΕΑΛΩ ΚVΙΑΣ; Nike as 464 but to r., palm tree.
475. Æ ↑ 7.63. *Rev.* ΙΟVΔΑΙΑΣΕΑΛ ѠΚVΙΑΣ.
476. Æ ↑ 7.74. *Rev.* countermark as 463.

Obv. ΑVΤΟΚΡΤΙΤ ΟΣΚΑΙΣΑΡ.
Rev. ΙΟΥΔΑΙΑΣ ΕΑΛѠΚVΙΑΣ (477–80) or ΙΟVΔΑΙϹ-ΕΑΛѠΚVΙΑϹ (481–83). Trophy; to l., Jewess (Judaea) seated l., mourning; to r., shield.

477. Æ ↑ 12.45.
478. Æ ↑ 13.07.

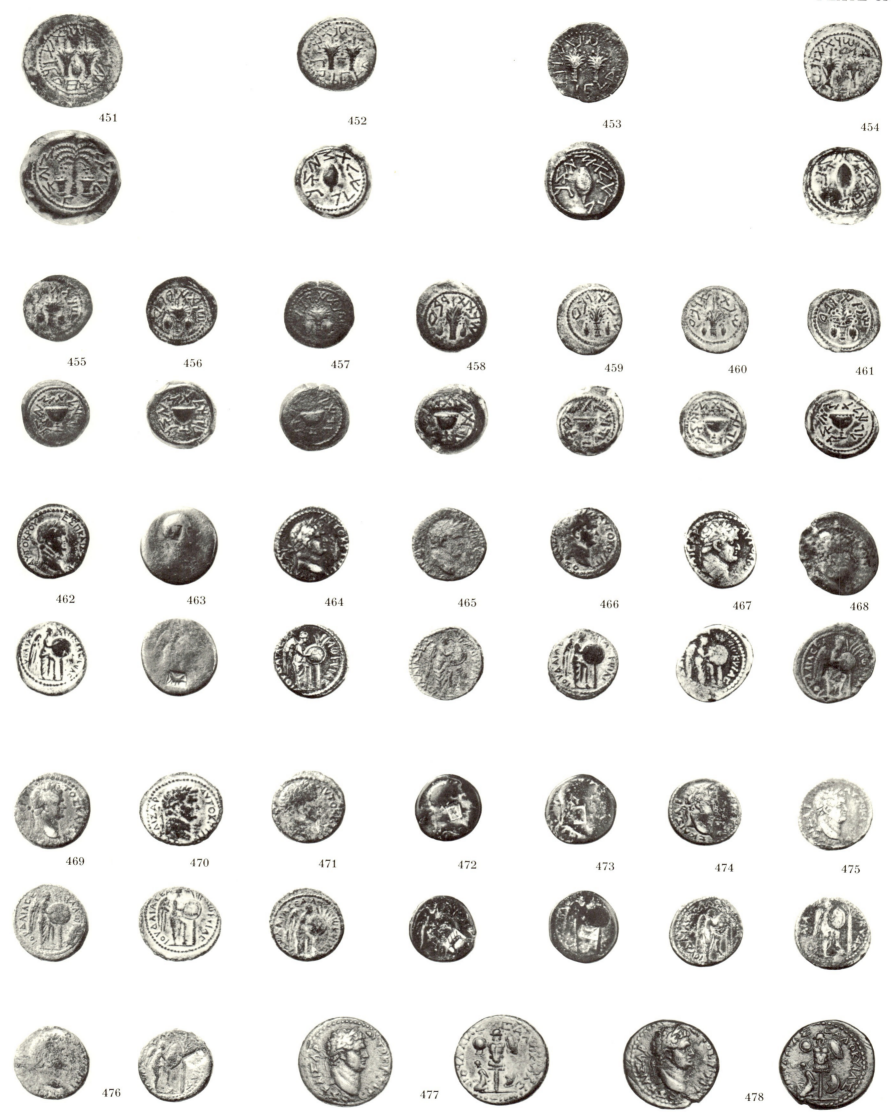

451 452 453 454

455 456 457 458 459 460 461

462 463 464 465 466 467 468

469 470 471 472 473 474 475

476

477

478

479

480

481

482

483

484

485

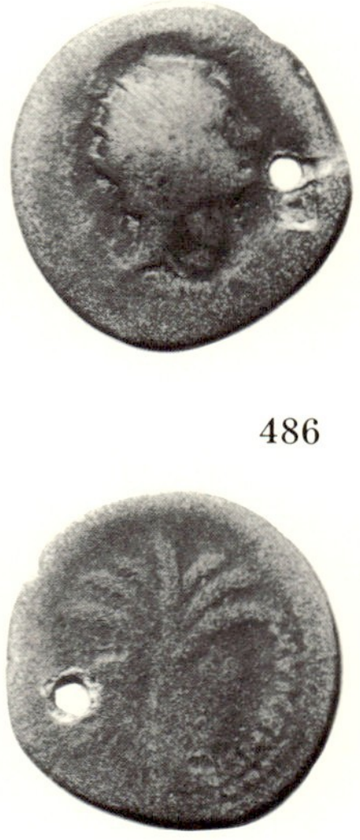
486

487

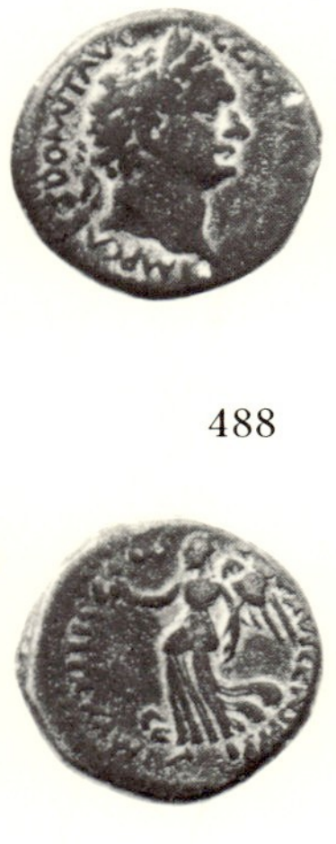
488

489

490

491

492

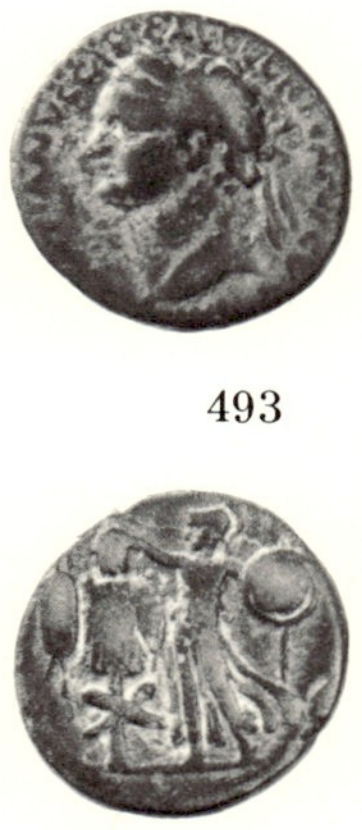
493

494

495

496

497

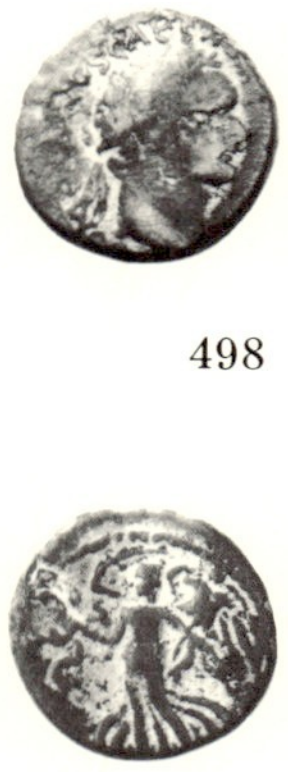
498

499

500

JEWISH COINS: JUDAEA CAPTA (cont.)

479. Æ ↑ 11.57.
480. Æ ↑ 13.72.
481. Æ ↑ 12.27.
482. Æ ↑ 11.90.
483. Æ ↑ 12.13. *Obv.* countermark as 472.

ROMAN ADMINISTRATION UNDER DOMITIAN

Mint of Caesarea

Obv. IMPCAESDOMITAVGGERMPMTRPXI Radiate head of Domitian r.

Rev. IMPXXI COSXVI CENSPPP Palm tree. A.D. 91/2.

484. Æ ↑ 16.26.
485. Æ ↑ 15.80. *Obv.* countermark: head (Nerva?).
486. Æ ↑ 12.51. Pierced. *Obv.* countermark as 485.

Obv. IMPCAESDOMITAVGGERMTRPXII Laureate head of Domitian r.

Rev. IMPXXIIIC OS XVICENSPPP Nike advancing l., holding wreath and trophy. A.D. 93.

487. Æ ↑ 12.82.
488. Æ ↑ 13.27.
489. Æ ↑ 9.52. *Obv.* countermark: head (Nerva or Trajan?).

Obv. IMPDOMITIANVSCAESAVGGERMANICVS (sometimes incompletely preserved). Laureate head of Domitian r. (490–91, 495–500), or l. (492–94).

Rev. Minerva standing r. on galley, holding spear and shield; to l., trophy; to r., small owl.

490. Æ ↑ 16.64.
491. Æ ↑ 12.97.

Rev. Athena advancing l., resting r. hand on trophy; holding shield and spear in l.

492. Æ ↑ 10.31.
493. Æ ↑ 8.73.
494. Æ ↑ 11.71. Doublestruck.

Rev. type as 487.

495. Æ ↑ 5.29.
496. Æ ↑ 5.12.
497. Æ ↑ 5.02.
498. Æ ↑ 5.08.

Rev. VICTOR AVG Trophy.

499. Æ ↑ 5.41.
500. Æ ↑ 5.46.

JEWISH COINS: BAR COCHBA WAR (A.D. 132–35)

The vine leaf (nos. 506–11, 526–43, 566–79) and the bunch of grapes (513–16, 521, 525, 544–45, 553–54, 556, 558, 561–65 585–92) have been turned upward so that the relative position to each other of the die axis and the inscription conforms to that of other coins of this section.

Practically all coins of this group are overstruck on previous issues. On all specimens, obv. and rev. types are enclosed within a circular dotted border.

Obv. Palaeo-Hebrew inscription = YRWŠLM (Jerusalem). Tetrastyle temple at Jerusalem; within, ark (?).
Rev. Palaeo-Hebrew inscription = ŠNT' ḤTLG' LTYŚR' L, year 1 of the redemption of Israel (A.D. 132). Lulav; to l., ethrog.
Tetradrachm.

501. AR ↑ 12.32. Glendining, 30 Nov. 1937, 31.

Obv. Palaeo-Hebrew inscription = ŠM'WN / N ŚY' / YSR'L (Shimon, prince of Israel), within wreath.
Rev. Inscription as 501. Amphora.

502. Æ ↑ 24.90.
503. Æ ↑ 22.73.
504. Æ ↑ 16.11.
505. Æ ↑ 19.43. *Obv.* inscription similar to 501, but YRW / ŠLM within wreath. Ex Pozzi coll.

Obv. Inscription as 502. Date palm.
Rev. Inscription as 501. Vine leaf.

506. Æ ↑ 11.65. *Obv.* ŠM'WN / NŚY' / YŚR'L / Ś The addition of the last letter, Ś, in the obv. inscription is an error.
507. Æ ↑ 11.14. *Obv.* inscription similar to 505.
508. Æ ↑ 16.75.
509. Æ ↑ 7.31.
510. Æ ↑ 13.19. The rev. shows traces of countermark on coin over which 510 was struck: head (emperor?). See 485.
511. Æ ↑ 16.76. Crude style; obv. inscription incomplete.

Obv. Inscription as 502. Palm branch within wreath.
Rev. Inscription as 501. Harp with six strings.

512. Æ ↑ 8.34.

Obv. Palaeo-Hebrew inscription = 'L' / ZNRH / KH [*sic*] (Eleazar the priest). Date palm.
Rev. Inscription as 501, but the last two letters are missing. Bunch of grapes.

513. Æ ↑ 5.82.
514. Æ ↑ 4.03.
515. Æ ↑ 4.86. Inscription retrograde.
516. Æ ↑ 7.92. Inscription retrograde.

Obv. Inscription as 501 (517–18) or Palaeo-Hebrew inscription = ŠM'WN (Shimon) (519). Tetrastyle temple as 501.
Rev. Palaeo-Hebrew inscription = ŠBLḤRYŚR'L, y[ear] 2 of the free[dom] of Israel (A.D. 133). Lulav; to l., ethrog.
Tetradrachms.

517. AR ↑ 14.35. Obv. die as 501. Hebron hoard of 1924.
518. AR ↑ 14.68. *Obv.* inscription similar to 501, but to l. and r., YRW ŠLM; first letter retrograde. Temple on podium decorated with vertical lines; above, rosette or star.
519. AR ↑ 14.84. *Obv.* type as 518.

Denarii.

The following coins (520–25) bear variations of the obv. inscription as 519 and rev. inscription as 517.

Obv. ŠM / ' within wreath.
Rev. ŠBLḤRYŚ[R' L]. Jug with handle; to r., palm branch.

520. AR ↗ 3.51. Traces of Latin inscription: ... HADRIAN... on Roman denarius undertype.

Obv. ŠM'WN. Bunch of grapes.
Rev. As 520.

521. AR ↓ 2.23. Traces of head of emperor (Vespasian?).

Obv. ŠM / N'W [*sic*], within wreath.
Rev. ŠBLḤRYŚ'L [*sic*]. Lyre with three strings.

522. AR ↑ 2.99.

501 502 503 504 505

506 507 508 509 510 511

512 513 514 515 516

517 518 519 520 521 522

523 524 525 526 527 528 529

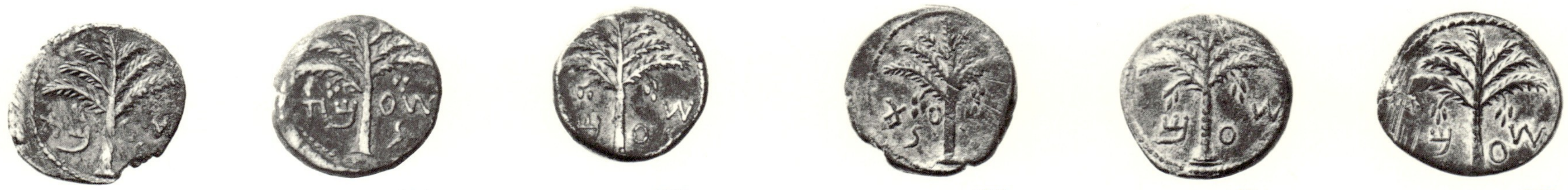

530 531 532 533 534 535

536 537 538 539 540 541

542 543 546 547

544 545

JEWISH COINS: BAR COCHBA WAR (cont.)

Obv. As 521.
Rev. As 522.

523. AR ↑ 3.36.

Obv. As 522.
Rev. ŠBLḤRYŚR'L Palm branch.

524. AR ↑ 3.18. Recut die. Clear traces of head of emperor (Nero ?).

Obv. As 521.
Rev. As 524, but letter, R, missing in last word of inscription.

525. AR ↑ 3.41. Naville 12, 18 Oct. 1926, 2030.

Obv. Inscription as 519, but with letters variously distributed. Date Palm.
Rev. Inscription as 517 but ŠBLḤRŚYR'L. Vine leaf.

Note disorder of letters in last word. Because 526–45 have been so badly struck, it has been decided to include pairs of die duplicates (538–39) and 544–45).

526. Æ ↑ 11.81.
527. Æ ↑ 7.32.
528. Æ ↑ 12.62. *Rev.* die of 527.
529. Æ ↑ 12.09. Possibly rev. die of 527.
530. Æ ↑ 8.48. *Obv.* ŠʿMW/N [*sic*].
531. Æ ↑ 10.97. *Rev.* die of 530.
532. Æ ↑ 12.10. *Rev.* die of 530.
533. Æ ↑ 10.34. *Rev.* die of 530.
534. Æ ↑ 10.74. ŠʿM [*sic*]. Probably rev. die of 530.
535. Æ ↑ 11.38.
536. Æ ↑ 9.22.
537. Æ ↑ 9.62. *Rev.* die of 536.
538. Æ ↑ 10.73. Probably obv. die of 537. Probably rev. die of 536.
539. Æ ↑ 8.62. Same dies as 538. *Obv.* undertype: clear traces of coin of Hadrian from Gaza (hand of Tyche holding scepter), with Greek inscription [Γ]AZA. See 914. *Rev.* undertype: clear head of Hadrian r.
540. Æ ↑ 10.58.
541. Æ ↑ 9.74. Crude style; some letters retrograde.
542. Æ ↑ 8.79. Crude style.
543. Æ ↑ 10.54. Very crude style. *Obv.* inscription retrograde.

Obv. Inscription as 501, but YRW / ŠLM. Date palm.
Rev. Inscription as 517, but ŠBLḤRYŚR'. Bunch of grapes.

544. Æ ↑ 4.27.
545. Æ ↑ 5.58. Same dies as 544.

The following coins (546–92), although undated, belong ca. A.D. 134/5.

Obv. As 519.
Rev. Palaeo-Hebrew inscription 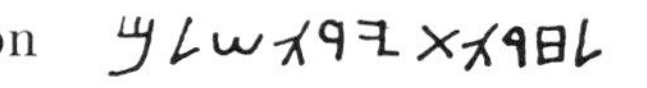
= LḤRWTYRWŠLM (for the freedom of Jerusalem). Lulav as 501.

Tetradrachms.

546. AR ↑ 14.71.
547. AR ↑ 14.52. *Obv.* undertype: clear traces of the head of Vespasian.

JEWISH COINS: BAR COCHBA WAR (cont.)

548. AR ↑ 14.10. *Obv.* die of 547; traces of Greek inscription on the undertype: ...NEPTRAIAN.... Hebron hoard of 1924.

549. AR ↑ 14.82. *Obv.* above temple, wavy line, and different style of inscription.

550. AR ↑ 14.32. As 549. *Obv.* die of 549. *Rev.* inscription somewhat crude; the letter, L, is missing. Hebron hoard of 1924.

Obv. ŠM'WN within wreath (551–52, 555, 557, 559–60) or around bunch of grapes (553–54, 556, 558, 561–65).

Rev. Inscription as 546, sometimes poorly preserved or abbreviated. Jug with handle (551–54), palm branch (555–56), two trumpets (557–58) or lyre with three strings (559-65).

Denarii.

551. AR ↑ 3.31. *Obv.* ŠM / 'NW [*sic*]. *Rev.* to r., palm branch. Overstruck on a Roman denarius of Domitian: *Obv.* [IMPCAESDO]MITAVGGERMPMTRPXI Laureate head of Domitian r. *Rev.* CENSPPP Minerva advancing r., holding spear and shield (struck in A.D. 91).

552. AR ↑ 3.04. *Obv.* die of 522.

553. AR ↑ 3.11. *Rev.* as 551.

554. AR ↑ 2.74.

555. AR ↑ 3.10.

556. AR ↑ 3.60.

557. AR ↑ 2.94. *Obv.* die of 551. Ex Sir Arthur Evans coll.

558. AR ↑ 2.87. Crude style. *Rev.* undertype: Traces of head of Trajan and inscription ...NAVG....

559. AR ↗ 3.18. *Obv.* ŠM / N'W [*sic*].

560. AR ↑ 3.16.

561. AR ↑ 3.04. *Obv.* undertype: traces of head of Trajan and inscription.

562. AR ↑ 3.11. *Obv.* undertype: traces of NERV....

563. AR ↑ 3.51. *Obv.* undertype: traces of the provincial denarius of Trajan and CEBΓEPMΔAK; *Rev.* XE ΞΠVAT.

564. AR ↗ 3.40.

565. AR ↑ 3.02. Very crude style.

Obv. Inscription as 519, but ŠM 'W / N. Date Palm.

Rev. Inscription as 546. Vine leaf.

566. Æ ↑ 9.78.

567. Æ ↑ 10.41. *Rev.* die of 566.

568. Æ ↑ 10.50. *Rev.* die of 566.

569. Æ ↑ 9.70. *Rev.* die of 566.

570. Æ ↑ 9.38.

571. Æ ↑ 9.77. *Rev.* die of 570.

572. Æ ↑ 11.30. *Rev.* die of 570.

573. Æ ↑ 10.76.

574. Æ ↑ 8.16.

575. Æ ↑ 9.30.

576. Æ ↑ 9.42.

577. Æ ↑ 11.21.

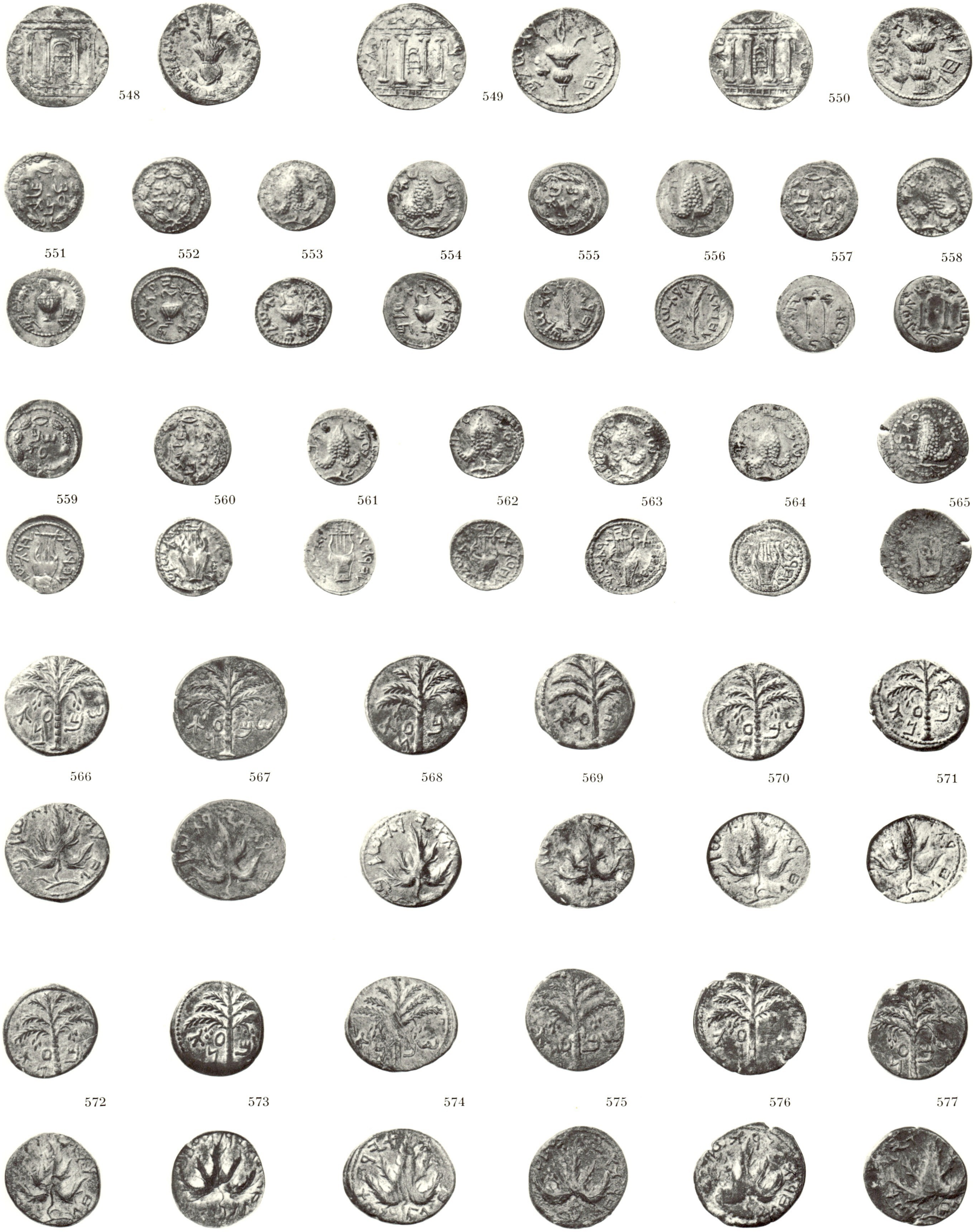

548 549 550

551 552 553 554 555 556 557 558

559 560 561 562 563 564 565

566 567 568 569 570 571

572 573 574 575 576 577

578

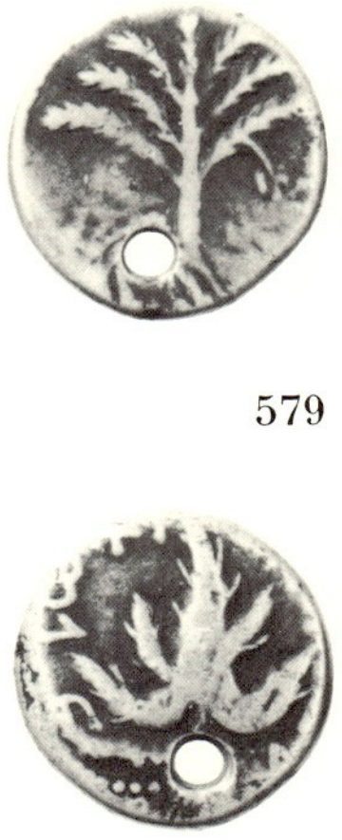
579

580

581

582

583

584

585

586

587

588

589

590

591

592

593

594

595

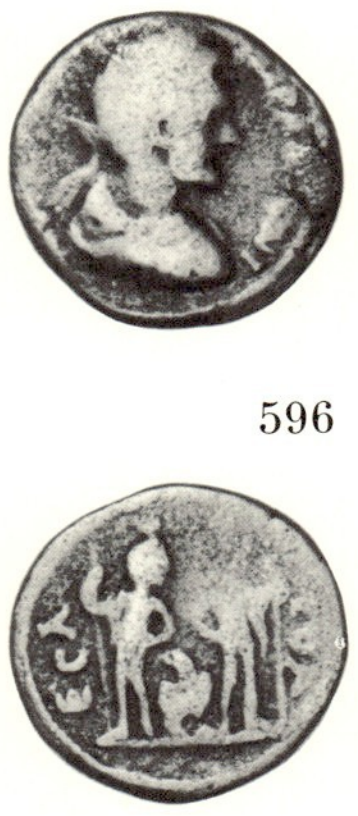
596

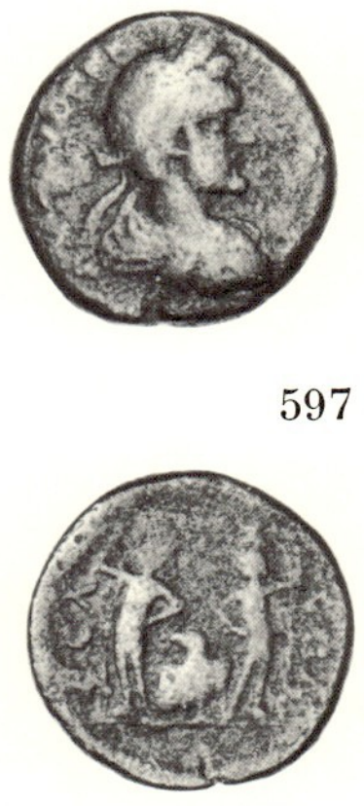
597

598

599

600

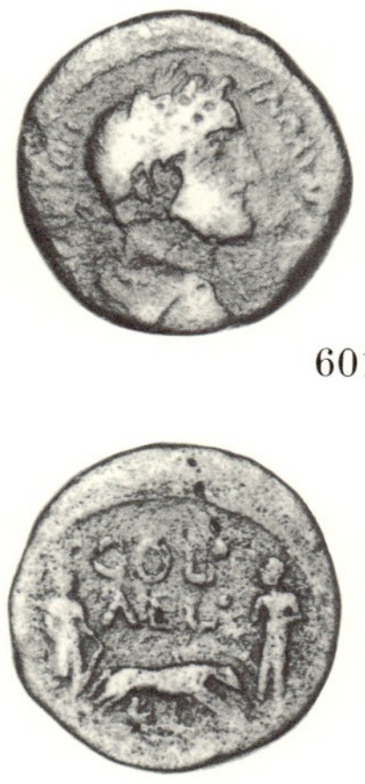
601

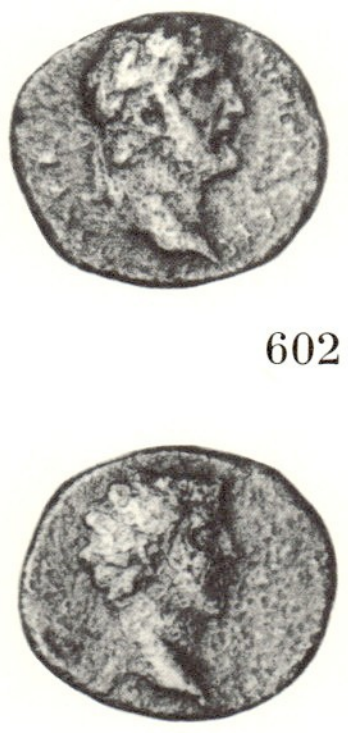
602

603

604

605

606

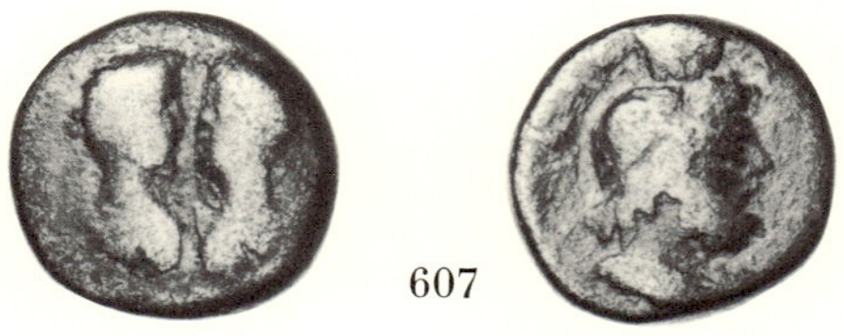
607

JEWISH COINS: BAR COCHBA WAR (cont.)

578. Æ ↑ 10.63. *Rev.* die of 577.
579. Æ ↑ 10.07. Pierced.

Obv. Inscription as 519, sometimes incompletely preserved. Lyre with three strings.
Rev. Inscription as 546. Palm branch within wreath.

580. Æ ↑ 5.48.
581. Æ ↑ 5.95.
582. Æ ↑ 5.97.
583. Æ ↑ 7.35.
584. Æ ↑ 5.54. *Obv.* to r., uncertain motif (▭ ?).

Obv. Inscription as 501, but YRW / ŠLM (585-86) or as 519, but ŠMʿW/N. Palm tree.
Rev. Inscription as 546. Bunch of grapes.

585. Æ ↑ 4.26.
586. Æ ↑ 3.92.
587. Æ ↑ 5.42.
588. Æ ↑ 4.68.
589. Æ ↑ 4.58.
590. Æ ↑ 4.53.
591. Æ ↑ 4.11.
592. Æ ↑ 6.24. ŠMʿ/NW [*sic*].

C. PROVINCIAL CITY COINS

Bellinger references are to the coins listed in A. R. Bellinger, *The Syrian Tetradrachms of Caracalla and Macrinus*, ANSNS 3 (New York, 1940).

The Homs Hoard of 1936 and the Khirbet el Atmaniyeh Hoard of 1937, given as provenances for certain coins in this section, are too late in date for inclusion in Noe's *Bibliography* or the *IGCH*. Lists of contents are on file at the ANS.

AELIA CAPITOLINA

Kadman references are to issues where the individual coins are illustrated in L. Kadman, *The Coins of Aelia Capitolina, Corpus Nummorum Palaestinensium* 1 (Jerusalem, 1956).

Antoninus Pius (A.D. 138–61)

Obv. IMPANTONINVSAVGPPP Head (593, 602) or draped bust (594–601) of Antoninus Pius r., laureate (594–602).
Rev. COLAE CAPIT Bust of Sarapis r.

593. Æ ↑ 10.22. *Obv.* IMPCTAELANT.

Rev. CAC (partially preserved, in exergue). Tetrastyle temple with central arch; within, Tyche standing l., holding small bust and scepter.

594. Æ ↑ 11.63. Kadman 12 (rev. only).

Rev. COA ECA Nude Dioscuri standing facing, looking at each other; in center, eagle.

595. Æ ↑ 12.67.
596. Æ ↑ 8.87. *Obv.* die of 595.
597. Æ ↑ 9.28.

Rev. CO·AE CA Bust of Tyche r.

598. Æ ↓ 9.95.
599. Æ ↑ 6.77.
600. Æ ↓ 7.00.

Rev. COL·/AEL·/CAP She-wolf r., suckling Romulus and Remus, flanked by Dioscuri.

601. Æ ↑ 10.23.

Rev. MAVP.... Head of M. Aurelius r.

602. Æ ↓ 4.87.

Marcus Aurelius and Lucius Verus (A.D. 161–69)

Obv. IMPCAESANTONINOETVERO Confronted busts of M. Aurelius and L. Verus, draped and laureate.
Rev. COL AEL CAP Tyche seated l., holding patera and cornucopiae.

603. Æ ↓ 15.18.
604. Æ ↓ 16.01. *Obv.* probably die of 603.

Rev. COL AEL.... Nike advancing l., holding wreath and palm branch.

605. Æ ↑ 15.30.

Obv. IMPCAESMAVREL ANTONINVSAVG Laureate head of M. Aurelius r.
Rev. LVCIVS VERVS A[VG] Laureate head of L. Verus r.

606. Æ ↑ 8.54. Kadman 62.

Marcus Aurelius and Commodus

Obv. Traces of inscription. Confronted busts of M. Aurelius and Commodus, draped and laureate.
Rev. [C]OLAE.... Bust of Sarapis l.

607. Æ ↑ 15.82.

PROVINCIAL CITY COINS: AELIA CAPITOLINA (cont.)

Lucius Verus (A.D. 161–69)

Obv. Draped bust of L. Verus r., laureate.
Rev. COL AEL CAP Sarapis seated l., holding scepter and extending hand over Cerberus.

608. Æ ↑ 19.93. *Obv.* IMPCAESL·AV RELVERVSAVG Kadman 70 (obv. only).

Rev. Draped bust of Faustina Junior r.

609. Æ ↑ 14.98. *Obv.* IMPCAESL·AVR.... *Rev.* FAVSTINA AVGVSTA·C·A·C.

610. Æ ↓ 8.04. *Obv.* IMPCSL·AVR VERVSAVG *Rev.* FAVSTINA AVGVST C A C. Kadman 53, erroneously published as a coin of Marcus Aurelius. The coin is the half denomination of 609.

Commodus (A.D. 177–92)

Obv. Traces of inscription. Draped bust of Commodus r., laureate.
Rev. COL AEL Tetrastyle temple with central arch; within, Tyche standing l., holding small bust and scepter.

611. Æ ↓ 13.38. *Obv.* illegible inscription.

Rev. COLA ELCAP Bust of Tyche r.

612. Æ ↓ 24.09. *Obv.* ...AVRCOM....

Rev. COLAE LCAP Bust of Sarapis r.

613. Æ ↑ 17.05. *Obv.* ...COMMODV....

Caracalla (A.D. 198–211)

Obv. AYTKAIANT WNINOCCЄ Draped bust of Caracalla r., laureate.
Rev. ΔΗΜΑΡΧЄ ΞΥΠΑΤΟCΤΟΔ Eagle standing facing on thyrsus, wings spread, head l., holding wreath in beak.

Tetradrachms.

614. AR ↓ 13.76. *Rev.* to l., cantharus; between eagle's legs, bunch of grapes. Bellinger 353.1. A.D. 215–17.

615. AR ↓ 11.23. *Rev.* between eagle's legs, cantharus. Bellinger 356.1. A.D. 215–17.

Macrinus (A.D. 217–18)

Obv. IMPCCOPMA CRINVSAVG Draped bust of Macrinus r., laureate.
Rev. COLC AP CO MM/AELIA Tetrastyle temple with central arch; within, Tyche standing l., holding small bust and scepter; between columns, two figures of Nike.

616. Æ ↑ 9.26. Kadman 98.

Diadumenian (A.D. 218)

Obv. ΜΟΠΑΝΤWΝ ΚΑΙ Draped bust of Diadumenian r.
Rev. ΔΗΜΑΡΧЄ ΞΥΠΑΤΟC Eagle standing facing on thyrsus, wings spread, head r., holding wreath in beak; between legs, cantharus.

Tetradrachm.

617. AR ↑ 10.35. Bellinger 360.1. A.D. 217/8.

Obv. MOPDIADVMENIANVSC Draped bust of Diadumenian r.
Rev. COLAELC COMMPF Bust of Sarapis r.

618. Æ ↑ 7.57.

Elagabalus (A.D. 218–22)

Obv. Draped bust of Elagabalus r., laureate (619–22, 624–26) or radiate (623).
Rev. Tyche standing l., holding scepter and sacrificing at altar; r. foot resting on helmet (?); to l., standard with legionary eagle; in exergue, chalice.

619. Æ ↑ 8.65. *Obv.* IMCMAV ANTO.... *Rev.* ...ACC PF.

620. Æ ↑ 9.03. Inscriptions not preserved.

621. Æ ↑ 9.75. *Obv.* ...ANTONI.... *Rev.* inscription not preserved.

Rev. COL·AEL·CA·CPF Mounted Dioscuri l.; below, cantharus.

622. Æ ↑ 8.59. *Obv.* traces of inscription.

Rev. She-wolf r., suckling Romulus and Remus.

623. Æ ↑ 22.78. *Obv.* IMPCMAVRANTONINVSAVG *Rev.* COLAVRAEL CAPCOMM/PF.

624. Æ ↑ 13.85. *Obv.* ...AVR ΑИΤΟИΙИ. *Rev.* ...PF. Smaller denomination of 623.

Rev. Facing quadriga carrying the stone of Elagabalus; below, ivy branch.

625. Æ ↑ 6.78. *Obv.* IMPCMAVR ANTONINVS. *Rev.* ...CCPF Kadman 146.

626. Æ ↖ 7.79. *Obv.* as 625. *Rev.* inscription illegible.

Trajan Decius (A.D. 249–51)

Obv. Draped bust of T. Decius r., laureate.
Rev. COLAEL C APCOMPF Sarapis seated l., holding small bust and scepter; to l., small Cerberus.

627. Æ ↑ 7.13 (pierced). *Obv.* [IMP]CGMESQTRADECIVSAVG· Kadman 170.

Rev. COL.AEL.KAP.COM.... T. Decius and Herennius Etruscus standing facing each other, holding scepters and clasping hands.

628. Æ ↓ 12.29. *Obv.* IMPCGMESQTRADЄCIVSAVG. Kadman 172.

Herennia Etruscilla

Obv. HERENNIAETRVSCILLAAVG Bust of H. Etruscilla r.
Rev. COLAEL KCOMMPF Bust of Tyche r.

629. Æ ↑ 7.53. Hirsch 21, 16 Nov. 1908, 4319. Kadman 176.

Rev. COL/AELKAP/COMM/PF within wreath.

630. Æ ↑ 14.03. Kadman 180.

Herennius Etruscus

Obv. CHQDЄCIVSETRVSCVSAVG Draped bust of H. Etruscus r., radiate.
Rev. COL AEL C APCOMPF Sarapis standing r., holding scepter and small bust.

631. Æ ↑ 10.82. Kadman 184.

Hostilianus (A.D. 251)

Obv. GVALOSTMESQVINTVSCAE Draped bust of Hostilianus r., radiate.
Rev. She-wolf r., suckling Romulus and Remus.

632. Æ ↑ 17.83. *Rev.* ...AELKAP/COMMPF. Kadman 200.

633. Æ ↑ 13.57. *Obv.* die of 632. *Rev.* COL A ELKAP COMM; above, legionary standard with eagle. Kadman 201 (obv. only).

Rev. COLAELK...COMM.... Dionysus standing l., holding oenochoe and thyrsus; to l., panther.

634. Æ ↑ 14.29. *Obv.* die of 632.

608 609 610 611 612 613 614

615 616 617 618 619 620 621

622 623 624 625 626 627 628

629 630 631 632 633 634

635

636

637

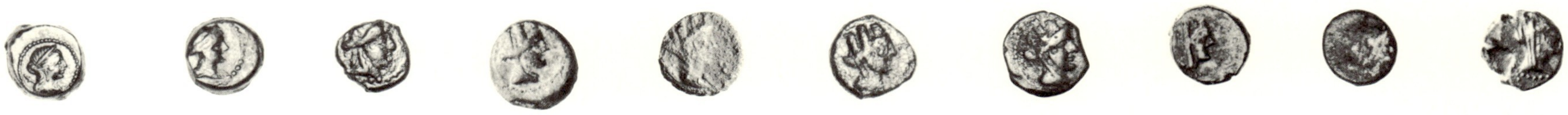

638 639 640 641 642 643 644 645 646 647

648 649 650 651 652

653

654 655 656 657 658 659 660

661 662 663 664 665 666 667 668

PROVINCIAL CITY COINS: ANTIPATRIS

Elagabalus (A.D. 218–22)

Obv. ΑΥΤ ΚΜΑΥΡΑΝΤѠΝΙ Draped bust of Elagabalus r., laureate.
Rev. . . . ΠΑΤΡΙC Tetrastyle temple; within, Tyche standing l., holding small bust and scepter.

635. Æ ↓ 6.87.

ASCALON

Era beginning 103 B.C., unless otherwise noted.

(Second Century B.C.)

Obv. Bust of Tyche r.
Rev. ΑΣ Prow of galley l.
Light hemidrachms.

636. AR ↑ 1.61. *Rev.* below, ⩚.
637. AR ↑ 1.54.

Obv. Bust of Aphrodite r.; to l., scepter.
Rev. ΑΣ Dove standing l.

638. Æ ↑ 1.85.
639. Æ ↑ 1.87.
640. Æ ↑ 1.50. Crude style.

Obv. Bust of Tyche r.
Rev. ΑΣ Prow of galley l.

641. Æ ↑ 2.17.
642. Æ ↑ 2.09.
643. Æ ↑ 2.14.
644. Æ ↑ 1.83.
645. Æ ↑ 2.22.
646. Æ ↑ 1.41. *Rev.* ΑΓ.
647. Æ ↑ 1.46. *Rev.* ΑΓ; below, Ι⊙ (date ?).

With Ptolemaic Portraits (first cent. B.C.)

Obv. Draped bust of Ptolemy XIII (?) r., diademed.
Rev. Eagle standing l. on fulmen; behind, palm branch; to l., dove.

Tetradrachms.

648. AR ↑ 13.46. *Rev.* ΑΣΚΑΛ. . .ΙΕΡΑΣΑΣΑΥΤ; below, ⋈; to r., L K (64 B.C.).
649. AR ↑ 14.09. *Rev.* ΑΣΚΑΛΩΝΙΤΩΝ ΙΕΡΑΣΑΣΥΑΥΤΟ; to l., ⚶; to r., LΑΛ (53 B.C.).

Obv. Draped bust of Ptolemy XV (?) r., diademed.

Tetradrachms.

650. AR ↑ 13.63. *Rev.* ΑΣΚΑΛΩΝΙΤΩΝ ΑΣΥΛΟΥΑΥΤΟΝΟ; to r., Μ̂Ι; to l., LM (44 B.C.).
651. AR ↑ 13.48. *Rev.* ΑΣΚΑΛΩΝΙΤ...ΑΣΥΛΟΥΑΥΤΟ; below, ⚶; to r., LM (44 B.C.).
652. AR ↑ 13.68. *Rev.* ΑΣΚΑΛΩΝΙ ΑΣΥΛΟΥΑΥΤΟ; below ⚶; to l., LMA (43 B.C.).

Autonomous (first cent. B.C.)

Obv. Head of Tyche r.
Rev. ΑΓ Eagle standing l.; behind, palm branch; to lower l., K; to r., ΛΕ (year 35).

Drachm.

653. AR ↑ 3.26. Cahn 71, 14 Oct. 1931, 581.

Obv. Head of Tyche r.
Rev. Eagle standing l; behind, palm branch; to l. LΓ over ΓΑ; to r., MA (43 B.C. ?).

Although they bear the inscription ΓΑ, 654–55 are apparently not from the mint of Gaza but from that of Ascalon, as they have all the characteristics of Ascalon coins of this time in types and style. The coins bear double dates, with the MA date apparently of the 84 B.C. era.

654. Æ ↑ 10.58.
655. Æ ↑ 9.94.

Rev. AC Galley l.

656. Æ ↑ 1.48.

Rev. AC Prow of galley l.

657. Æ ↑ 2.20. *Obv.* crude style.
658. Æ ↑ 1.53. *Obv.* as 657.

Rev. AC Winged caduceus; to r. and l., fillet (?).

659. Æ ↑ 2.60.

Rev. ΑΓ Galley 1.

660. Æ ↑ 3.37.

Obv. Laureate male head r.
Rev. ΑΣ Prow of galley 1.

Nos. 661 and 662, from the same obverse die, provide the key to the interpretation of the date on 661. 662's date NZ is clearly year 57, and it is impossible to read 661's date ΣΝ as year 250, 193 years apart. If the Σ on 661 is taken as a variant of Ϛ, 6, then the coin's date is year 56, or 48/7 B.C.).

661. Æ ↑ 3.74. *Rev.* below, ΣΝ (48/7 B.C.).
662. Æ ↑ 3.74. *Obv.* die of 661. *Rev.* below, NZ (47/6 B.C.).

Obv. Bust of Tyche r.
Rev. ΑΓ Galley l. (663–64) or r. (665).

663. Æ ↑ 3.25. *Rev.* at stern of galley, cruciform standard.
664. Æ ↑ 4.32. As 663.
665. Æ ↑ 4.07. *Rev.* on center of galley, symbol of Tanit.

Obv. Young male head r.
Rev. ΑΓ Double cornucopiae; in center, ear of corn (?).

666. Æ ↑ 2.01.

Augustus (31 B.C.–A.D. 14)

Obv. ...ΓΕ.... Head of Augustus r. (667) or l. (668).
Rev. ΑΓ/L/EP (A.D. 1/2). Tyche-Astarte standing l. on galley, holding scepter and aphlaston.

667. Æ ↑ 10.17.

Rev. ΑΓ Phanebal standing facing, holding sword and shield; behing shield, palm branch.

668. Æ ↑ 7.08.

PROVINCIAL CITY COINS: ASCALON (cont.)

Tiberius (A.D. 14–37)

Obv. ΣΕ Head of Tiberius r.; to r., sign of Tanit.
Rev. ΑΣ Phanebal standing facing, holding sword and shield; behind shield, palm branch.

669. Æ ↑ 6.12. *Rev.* to r., ΑΛΡ (A.D. 27/8).
670. Æ ↑ 7.66.

Caligula (A.D. 37–41)

Obv. Laureate head of Caligula l.
Rev. ΑΣΚΑΛΩ Tyche-Astarte standing l. on galley, holding scepter and aphlaston; to l., altar; to r., dove and ΒΜΡ (A.D. 38/9).

671. Æ ↑ 12.80.

Claudius (A.D. 41–54)

Obv. Laureate head of Claudius r. (672) or l. (673–74).
Rev. ΑΣΚΑΛΩ Tyche-Astarte standing l. on galley, holding scepter and aphlaston; to l., altar; to r., dove.

672. Æ ↑ 13.46. *Obv.* ΣΕΒΑΣΤΟΣ; countermark: head r. *Rev.* to r., ϚΜΡ (A.D. 42/3).
673. Æ ↑ 13.91. *Obv.* ΣΕΒΑΣΤΟΣ. *Rev.* to r., ϚΝΡ (A.D. 52/3) over ΒΡ.
674. Æ ↑ 12.23. As 673.

Nero (A.D. 54–67)

Obv. Head of Nero l. (r. on 677), laureate on 677–78.
Rev. ΑΣΚΑΛΩ Tyche-Astarte standing l. on galley, holding scepter and aphlaston; to l., altar; to r., dove.

675. Æ ↑ 13.38. *Rev.* to r., Β ΞΡ (A.D. 58/9).
676. Æ ↑ 8.64. *Obv.* ...ΤΟϹ. *Rev.* as 675.
677. Æ ↑ 12.79. *Obv.* ...ΤΟΣ. *Rev.* to r., ΑΟΡ (A.D. 67/8).
678. Æ ↑ 12.16. *Obv.* ΣΕΒΑΣΤΟΣ. *Rev.* to r., ΑΟΡ (A.D. 67/8).

Time of Vespasian

Obv. Head of Tyche r.
Rev. ΑΣ Galley sailing r., with cruciform standard at stern; above, ϚΟ̅Ρ (A.D. 72/3).

679. Æ ↑ 4.53.
680. Æ ↑ 5.05.
681. Æ ↑ 3.51.
682. Æ ↑ 4.38.

Rev. ΑΣ Galley sailing r.; above, Π̅Ρ (A.D. 76/7).

683. Æ ↑ 3.23.
684. Æ ↑ 3.86.
685. Æ ↑ 3.39.
686. Æ ↑ 4.49.
687. Æ ↑ 3.72.

Vespasian (A.D. 69–79)

Obv. ΣΕΒΑΣΤΟΣ, sometimes only partially preserved. Laureate head of Vespasian r.
Rev. ΑΣ Phanebal standing facing, holding sword and shield; behind shield, palm branch; to l., ϚΟΡ (A.D. 72/3).

688. Æ ↑ 7.71.
689. Æ ↑ 8.37.
690. Æ ↑ 7.87.

Obv. ΣΕ Laureate head of Vespasian (?) l.
Rev. ΑΣ Type as 688.

691. Æ ↑ 5.51.

Obv. Laureate head of Vespasian r.
Rev. ΑΣΚΑΛΩ Tyche-Astarte standing l. on galley, holding scepter and aphlaston; to l., altar; to r., star above dove.

692. Æ ↑ 14.75. *Obv.* ϹΕΒΑ...ΤΟϹ. *Rev.* to r., Π̅Ρ (A.D. 76/7).
693. Æ ↑ 12.31. *Obv.* ...ΤΟΣ. *Rev.* to r., Β Ρ (A.D. 78/9).

Time of Domitian

Obv. Head of Tyche r.
Rev. Galley sailing r.; above, ΗϤΡ (A.D. 94/5).

694. Æ ← 3.47.

Domitian (A.D. 81–98)

Obv. Laureate head of Domitian r.
Rev. ΑΣΚΑΛΩ Tyche-Astarte standing l. on galley, holding scepter and aphlaston; to l., altar; to r., dove.

695. Æ ↑ 9.51. *Rev.* to r., Ζ[ΠΡ] (A.D. 83/4).
696. Æ ↑ 11.76. *Obv.* ϹΕΒΑ...ΤΟϹ. *Rev.* to r., ΗΠΡ (A.D. 84/5).
697. Æ ↑ 9.35. *Rev.* to r., ΘΠΡ (A.D. 85/6).
698. Æ ↑ 11.78. *Obv.* ϹΕΒΑϹ; type l. *Rev.* as 697.
699. Æ ↑ 12.24. *Rev*, to r., ϤΡ over Λ (Α ?). If ϤΡ is the full date, the coin is dated to A.D. 86/7; if the lower letter is an Α, and is part of the date, the coin is dated to A.D. 87/8.

Rev. ΑϹ Phanebal standing facing, holding sword and shield; behind shield, palm branch; to l., ΗϤΡ (A.D. 94/5).

700. Æ ↑ 6.72. *Obv.* ϹΕΒΑϹ....
701. Æ ↑ 5.55. *Obv.* as 700.

Time of Trajan

Obv. ΑΣΚΑ Head of Tyche r.
Rev. Galley sailing r.

702. Æ ↑ 3.32. *Rev.* above, Ι̅Σ̅ (A.D. 106/7).
703. Æ ↑ 2.92. *Rev.* above, Ε̅Ι̅Ϲ̅ (A.D. 112/3).

669 670 671 672 673 674 675

676 677 678 679 680 681 682 683

684 685 686 687 688 689 690 691

692 693 694 695 696 697 698

699 700 701

702

703

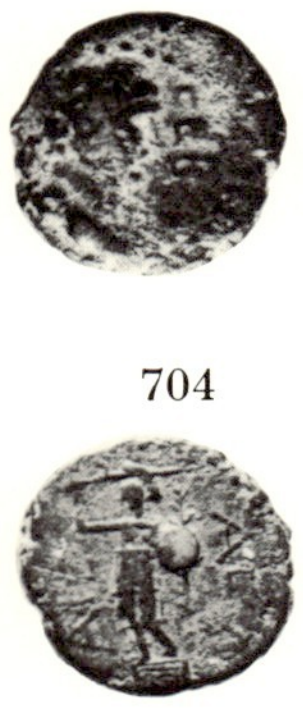
704

705

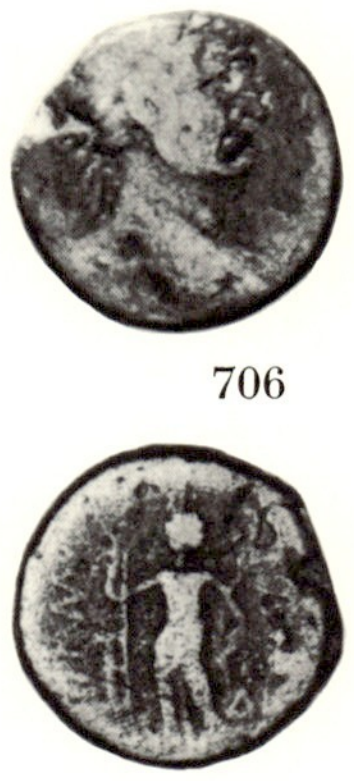
706

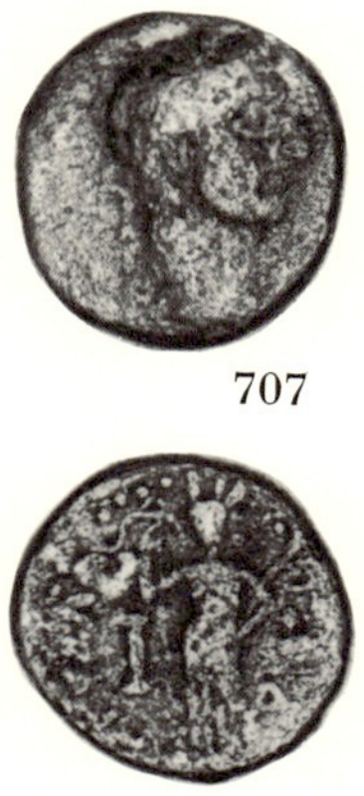
707

708

709

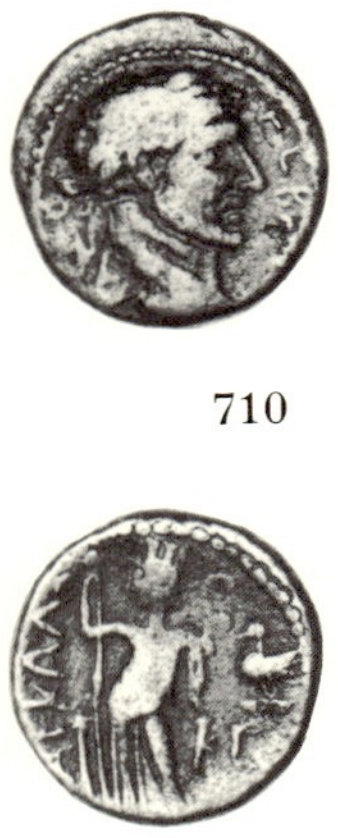
710

711

712

713

714

715

716

717

718

719

720

721

722

723

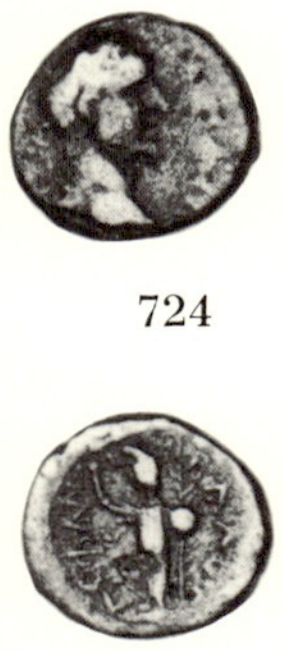
724

725

726

727

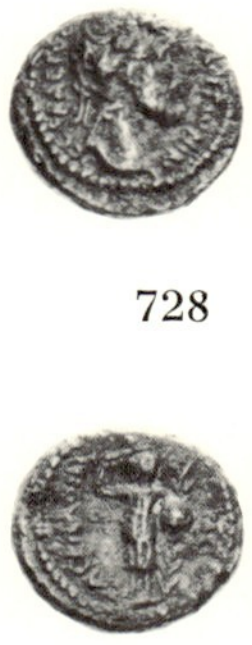
728

729

730

731

732

733

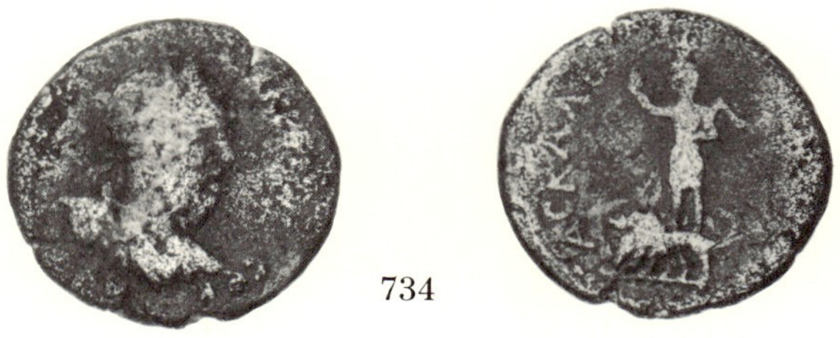
734

735

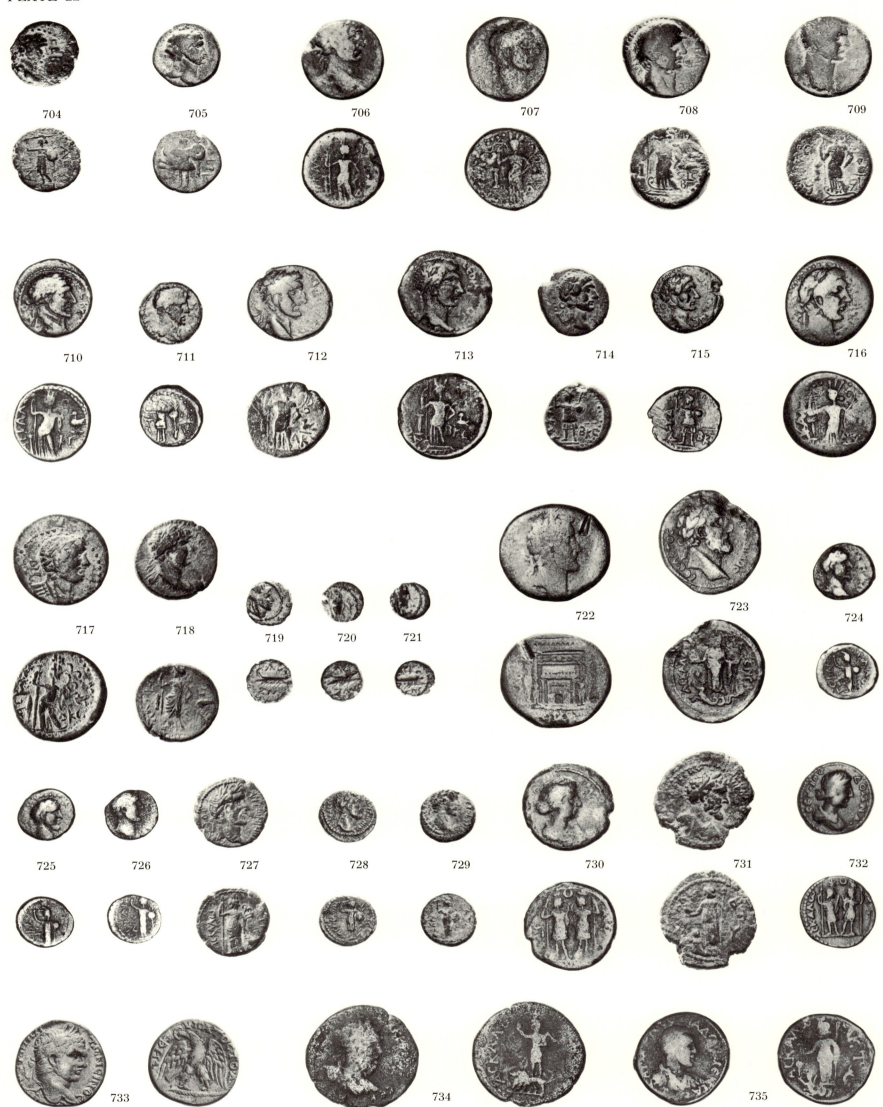

PROVINCIAL CITY COINS; ASCALON (cont.)

Trajan (A.D. 98–117)

Obv. Laureate head of Trajan r.
Rev. AL Phanebal standing facing, holding sword and shield; behind shield, palm branch.

704. Æ ↑ 5.32. *Obv.* LEBA. *Rev.* to l., ΑΙL (A.D. 107/8).
705. Æ ↑ 5.33. *Obv.* probably as 704. *Rev.* date not preserved.

Rev. ACKAΛO, sometimes only partially preserved. Tyche-Astarte standing l. on galley, holding scepter and aphlaston; to l., altar; to r., dove.

706. Æ ↑ 12.37. *Rev.* to r., ΔΙC (A.D. 110/1).
707. Æ ↑ 11.47. As 706.

Obv. CЄBACTOS, often only partially preserved. Type as 704.
Rev. Inscription and type as 706.

708. Æ ↑ 14.21. *Rev.* to r., ϚΙC (A.D. 113/4) over BΠ.
709. Æ ↑ 11.11. As 708, but no BΠ (?).
710. Æ ↑ 9.90. *Rev.* to r., KL (A.D. 116/7).

Rev. Inscription and type as 704.

711. Æ ↑ 5.60. *Rev.* to r., KL (A.D. 116/7).

Rev. Inscription and type as 706.

712. Æ ↑ 11.67. *Rev.* to r., AKL (A.D. 117/8).

Hadrian (A.D.117–38)

Obv. LEBALTOL, sometimes incompletely preserved. Laureate head (713–16) or bust (717–18) of Hadrian r.
Rev. ALKAΛ..., sometimes incompletely preserved. Tyche-Astarte standing l. on galley, holding scepter and aphlaston; to l., altar; to r., dove.

713. Æ ↑ 11.82. *Rev.* to r., BKL (A.D. 118/9).

Rev. ALKA Phanebal standing facing, holding sword and shield; behind shield, palm branch.

714. Æ ↑ 6.68. *Rev.* to r., BKL (A.D. 118/9).
715. Æ ↑ 5.87. Dies of 714.

Rev. Inscription and type as 713.

716. Æ ↑ 9.97. *Rev.* to r., ΔKL (A.D. 120/1).
717. Æ ↑ 10.48. Doublestruck. As 716.
718. Æ ↑ 11.91. *Rev.* date not preserved. The fine style of the portrait of Hadrian indicates that the coin was apparently struck by the mint master of Gaza.

Time of Antoninus Pius

Obv. Head of Tyche r.
Rev. ACK Galley sailing r.

719. Æ ↑ 2.13. *Rev.* below, ZMC (A.D. 143/4).
720. Æ ↑ 1.63. As 719.
721. Æ ↑ 2.14. *Rev.* below, ЄNC (A.D. 151/2).

Antoninus Pius (A.D. 138–61)

Obv. Laureate head of Antoninus Pius r.
Rev. ACK.... Building with four doorways, the second from the outside with pillars shaped like human figures.

722. Æ ↑ 18.65. *Obv.* chisel cut; inscription illegible. *Rev.* in exergue, ΔNC (A.D. 150/1).

Rev. ACKAΛωN Derketo standing l. on triton holding cornucopiae; she holds dove and scepter, and has crescent above head.

723. Æ ↑ 16.11. *Obv.* [A]NTωNINOC CЄBACTOC. *Rev.* to r., ЄNC (A.D. 151/2).

Rev. AC Phanebal standing facing, holding sword and shield; behind shield, palm branch.

724. Æ ↑ 4.13. *Obv.* inscription illegible. *Rev.* to l. and r. ΦANHBAΛOC; to l., CNЄ (A.D. 151/2).
725. Æ ↑ 3.40. As 724.
726. Æ ↑ 3.19. As 724.

Obv. ANTωNINOC CЄBACTOS Type as 722.
Rev. ACKAΛω Tyche-Astarte standing l. on galley, holding scepter and aphlaston; to l., altar; to r., dove.

727. Æ ↑ 6.70. *Rev.* to r., ΞC (A.D. 156/7).

Rev. ACKAΛωN Type as 724.

728. Æ ↑ 3.66. *Rev.* to r., ΞC (A.D. 156/7).
729. Æ ↑ 3.78. *Rev.* to r., AΞC (A.D. 157/8).

Faustina II

Obv. ...NA AVΓ.... Bust of Faustina II r.
Rev. ACKAΛ Dioscuri standing facing, heads turned to look at each other, each holding spear and parazonium; above, crescent; to l., BΞC (A.D. 158/9).

730. Æ ↑ 12.72.

Septimius Severus (A.D. 193–211)

Obv. AYKΛCCЄOYHPOCCЄ.... Draped bust of S. Severus r., laureate.
Rev. ACKAΛω Derketo standing l. on triton holding cornucopiae; she holds dove and scepter, and has crescent above head; to r., BT (A.D. 198/9).

731. Æ ↑ 14.66.

Julia Domna

Obv. CЄB · IOY ΔOMNA · Draped bust of J. Domna r.
Rev. ACKAΛω Dioscuri standing facing, heads turned to look at each other, each holding spear and parazonium; above, crescent; to r., ΔT (A.D. 200/1).

732. Æ ↑ 7.87.

Caracalla (A.D. 198–217)

Obv. ...MAYAN TΩNЄINOC Laureate head of Caracalla r.
Rev. Eagle standing facing on palm branch, wings spread, head l., holding wreath in beak; in exergue, dove holding olive branch in beak; around, ΔHЄ Ξ YΠATOCTOΔ (A.D. 215–17).

733. Æ ↑ 11.68.

Macrinus (A.D. 217–18)

Obv. AV. . . MOΠ MAKPЄIN..CЄB Draped bust of Macrinus r., laureate.
Rev. ACKAΛω Isis (?) standing l. on three lions, holding scepter and flail; to r., traces of AKT (A.D. 217/8).

734. Æ ↑ 17.99.

Diadumenian (A.D. 218)

Obv. AY·M·OΠ...ΔIAΔOYMЄNIAN Draped bust of Diadumenian r.
Rev. ACKAΛω Derketo standing l. on triton holding cornucopiae; she holds dove and scepter, and has crescent above head; to r., AKT (A.D. 217/8).

735. Æ ↑ 12.27.

PROVINCIAL CITY COINS: ASCALON (cont.)

Diadumenian or Elagabalus

Obv. Illegible inscription. Draped bust r., laureate.
Rev. ACKAΛω Poseidon standing l., holding trident and extending r. arm; to lower l., dolphin (?); to r., traces of AKT (A.D. 217/8).

736. Æ ↑ 12.27. The obv. portrait is indeed similar to that of Diadumenian on 735, but may be an early portrait of Elagabalus. The date is common to both emperors.

Elagabalus (A.D. 218–22)

Obv. Draped bust of Elagabalus r., laureate.
Rev. ACKAΛω Derketo standing l. on triton holding cornucopiae; she holds dove and scepter, and has crescent above head; to r., AKT (A.D. 217/8).

737. Æ ↑ 12.40. *Obv.* ...MAY ANTωNєINOC.
738. Æ ↑ 10.80.

Rev. ACKAΛω Heracles, nude, standing l., holding ball (?) and club; to r., BK[T] (A.D. 218/9).

739. Æ ↑ 13.91. *Obv.* ... AV ANTωNIN....

Rev. ACKAΛU Building with four receding doorways, second from outside with pillars shaped like human figures; in exergue BKT (A.D. 218/9).

740. Æ ↑ 8.70. *Obv.* AYKMAANTωNєINOCCє.

Julia Maesa

Obv. IOVM AICAA Draped bust of J. Maesa r.
Rev. ACK AΛω Building with four receding doorways, second from outside with pillars shaped like human figures.

741. Æ ↑ 6.27.

Maximinus (A.D. 235–38)

Obv. Draped bust of Maximinus r., laureate.
Rev. CKAΛω [*sic*]. Bust of Isis l., over three lions' heads, and wearing atef-crown and holding scepter and flail; to r., HΛT (A.D. 234/5).

742. Æ ↓ 10.74. *Obv.* ...NOC.

Rev. Poseidon standing l., holding trident and extending r. arm; to r., possible traces of HΛT (A.D. 234/5).

743. Æ ↑ 11.97. *Obv.* MAΞIMєINO.

CAESAREA

Kadman references are to issues where the individual coins are illustrated in L. Kadman, *The Coins of Caesarea Maritima*, Corpus Nummorum Palaestinensium 2 (Jerusalem, 1957).

Claudius (A.D. 45–54)

Obv. CLAVDIVUS CAESARAVGPMTRPIMPPP Laureate head of Claudius r.
Rev. Anchor within wreath.

744. Æ ↑ 9.57.

Quasi-Autonomous

Obv. KAICAPEΩN Rudder.
Rev. Anchor; to l., and r., L IΔ (A.D. 68?).

745. Æ ↓ 2.80.

Obv. Bust of Tyche r., to l., LIΔ (A.D. 68?).
Rev. CE/BAC/TOC within wreath. The identification of this type with the mint of Caesarea is not certain.

746. Æ ↑ 3.17.
747. Æ ↑ 3.33.
748. Æ ↑ 3.05.
749. Æ ↑ 3.32.
750. Æ ↑ 3.39.
751. Æ ↑ 2.70.
752. Æ ↑ 3.53.

Nero (A.D. 54–67)

Obv. NEPΩN KAIΣAPΣEBAΣTOΣ Laureate head of Nero r.
Rev. KAIΣAPIA H ΠPOΣΣEBAΣTΩ ΛIMHNI Tyche standing l., holding bust and scepter; to l., LIΔ (A.D. 68).

753. Æ ↑ 11.27.
754. Æ ↑ 10.98.
755. Æ ↑ 10.26.
756. Æ ↑ 10.51. *Obv.* countermark XF of the Tenth Roman Legion, Fretensis.

Rev. KAIΣAPEωN Male figure standing r., holding spear and bust; to l., LIΔ (A.D. 68).

757. Æ ↑ 7.11. *Obv.* NEPωNΣEBAΣTOΣ.
758. Æ ↑ 5.81. *Obv.* inscription as 757.

Rev. EΠI/OV EΣΠA/ΣIANOV/ KAIΣAP/LIΔ within wreath (A.D. 68).

759. Æ ↑ 8.28. *Obv.* NEPωN....

Trajan (A.D. 98–117)

Obv. Laureate head of Trajan r.
Rev. C·I·F·AVG Tetrastyle temple; Tyche standing l. within, holding bust and scepter; in lower r., half-figure of harbor god. See 768, below.

760. Æ ↑ 27.31. *Obv.* IMPCAES NERTRAIANOOPAV.... *Rev.* Inscription barely visible in exergue.
761. Æ ↑ 11.79. *Obv.* As 760.

Rev. COLPRIFL.AVG.CAESARENSIS Emperor standing l., sacrificing over altar and holding cornucopiae.

762. Æ ↑ 13.80. *Obv.* IMPCAESNERT RAIANOOPAVGGERDACOSVIPP Kadman 23 (obv. only).
763. Æ ↑ 11.24. *Obv.* As 762.

Rev. COLPRIFL AVG CAESAR[E]N Nike advancing l., holding wreath and palm branch.

764. Æ ↑ 9.59. *Obv.* IMPCAESNERTRAIANOOPAVGGER....
765. Æ ↑ 7.78. *Obv.* as 764. Kadman 24.

736 737 738 739 740 741 742 743

744 745 746 747 748 749 750 751 752

753 754 755 756 757 758 759

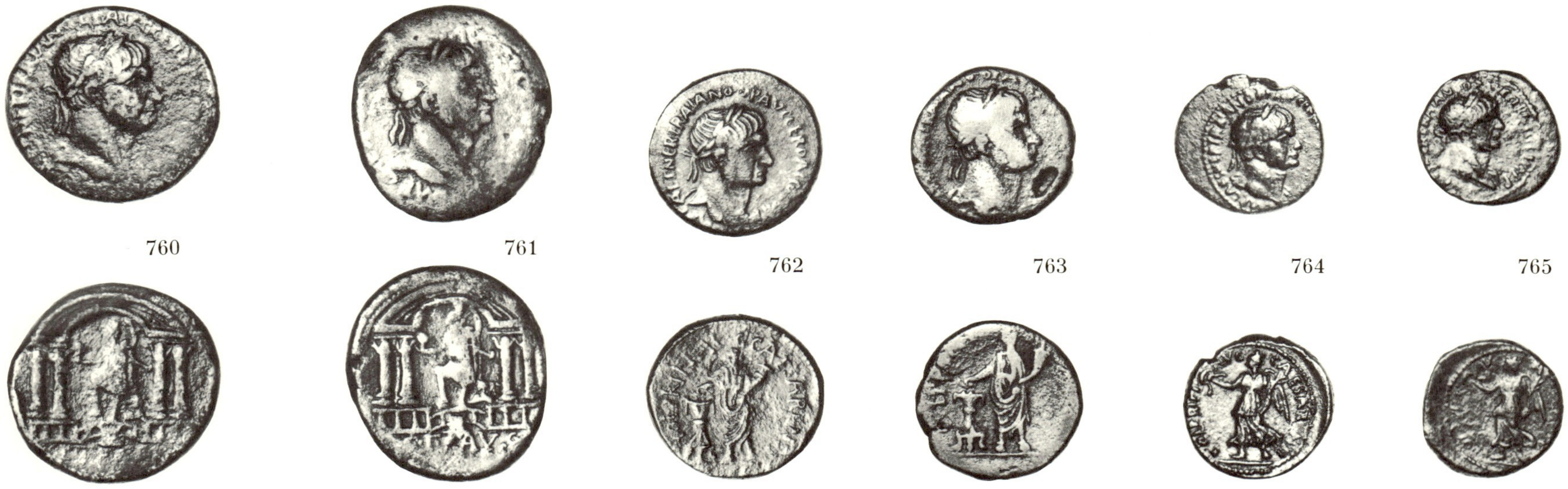

760 761 762 763 764 765

766 767 768 769 770 771 772

773 774 775 776 777 778 779

780 781 782 783 784 785

786 787 788 789 790 791

PROVINCIAL CITY COINS: CAESAREA (cont).

Hadrian (A.D. 117–38)

Obv. Draped bust of Hadrian r., laureate.
Rev. COLIFLAVG CAESAREN Founder ploughing r.; above, small Nike.

766. Æ ↑ 10.98. *Obv.* IMPTRAHADRIANO.

Rev. COLIFLAVG/CAESAREN Bust of Sarapis r.

767. Æ ↑ 13.29. *Obv.* IANOCAES.

Rev. CIFAVGCAESAR Tyche standing l., holding bust and scepter, r., foot resting on harbor god.

For discussion of the harbor god, see J. Ringel, "La Fortune de Cesarée..." *RN* 1974, pp. 155–59. The actual statue has recently been excavated at Caesarea.

768. Æ ↑ 9.28. *Obv.* IMPTRAHADRIANOCA Kadman 26.
769. Æ ↑ 10.18. *Obv.* IMPTRAHADRIANOCAAVG.
770. Æ ↑ 8.11. *Obv.* as 769.

Rev. CIF AVG CAESAR Apollo standing l., holding serpent; to r., tripod.

771. Æ ↑ 5.66. *Obv.* IMPTRAHADRIANOCAE Kadman 29 (rev. only).
772. Æ ↑ 5.56. *Obv.* as 771. Kadman 29 (obv. only).

Rev. CIFAC Lion advancing r.; above, serpent.

773. Æ ↑ 2.29. *Obv.* as 771.
774. Æ ↑ 2.88. *Obv.* as 771.
775. Æ ↑ 2.51. *Obv.* as 771.

Marcus Aurelius (A.D. 161–80)

Obv. Draped bust of M. Aurelius r., laureate.
Rev. COLPRIMAFL AVGCAESAREA Bust of Sarapis r.

776. Æ ↑ 12,02. *Obv.* AVRELIOCAESANTONINAVGPF.
777. Æ ↑ 11.91. *Obv.* ...ONINVS.....
778. Æ ↑ 13.63. *Obv.* IMPCAESMAVRANTONINVS.
779. Æ ↖ 9.73. *Obv.* as 778.

Rev. COLPRIMAFLAVGVSCAESAREA Nike advancing l., holding wreath and palm branch.

780. Æ ↑ 8.63. *Obv.* IMPCAESARANTONINVSAVG.

Faustina II

Obv. FAVSTINAAVGVSTA Draped bust of Faustina r.
Rev. COLPRIMAFLAVGCAESAREA Emperor standing l., holding cornucopiae, sacrificing with phiale over altar.

781. Æ ↑ 11.69. Kadman 50.

Lucius Verus (A.D. 161–69)

Obv. IMPCAESLAVRVERVSAVG.... Draped bust of L. Verus r.
Rev. COLPRIMAFLAVGVSCAESARE.... Bust of Sarapis r.

782. Æ ↑ 15.68.

Commodus (A.D. 177–92)

Obv. IMCOMMODVSANTONINVS Draped bust of Commodus r.
Rev. COLPRIMAFAVGCAESAREA Bust of Sarapis r.

783. Æ ↑ 11.75. Kadman 59.
784. Æ ↑ 11.28. *Obv.* die of 783.
785. Æ ↑ 11.03.

Caracalla (A.D. 198–217)

Obv. AYTKAIANTWNINOCCЄ Bust of Caracalla r., laureate.
Rev. ΔΗΜΑΡΧЄΞVΠΑΤΟCΤΟΔ Eagle, head l., standing facing on torch entwined by serpent.

Tetradrachms.

786. AR ↑ 13.43. Khirbet el Atmaniyeh hoard of 1937. Bellinger 363.10.
787. AR ↓ 13.73. Homs hoard of 1936. Bellinger 363.9.
788. AR ↓ 14.52. Khirbet el Atmaniyeh hoard of 1937. Bellinger 363.11.
789. AR ↑ 12.99. *Rev.* between legs of eagle, bull's head r. Bellinger 365.6.
790. AR ↑ 12.60. *Rev.* as 789. Khirbet el Atmaniyeh hoard of 1937. Bellinger 367.1.
791. AR ↑ 13.14. *Rev.* between legs of eagle, dot within circle.

PROVINCIAL CITY COINS: CAESAREA

Caracalla (cont.)

Obv. Draped bust of Caracalla r., laureate (792–93, 795) or radiate (794).
Rev. SPQR within wreath supported by eagle.

792. Æ ↑ 12.59. Very worn; inscriptions illegible. Khirbet el Atmaniyeh hoard of 1937.
793. Æ ↓ 6.27. *Obv.* KAIM.AV...; *Rev.* CIFAFCCAESMET....

Rev. COLIFLAVGFCCAESAREA Bust of Sarapis r.

794. Æ ↑ 8.29. *Obv.* IMPCMAVRANT....

Rev. COIFL / AVFC Founder ploughing r.

795. Æ ↑ 9.80. *Obv.* IMP....NINVS.

Macrinus (A.D. 217–18)

Obv. AVTKAIMOΠCЄOMAKPINOC Draped bust of Macrinus r., laureate.
Rev. ΔHMAPXЄΞYΠATOCΠΠ Eagle, head l., standing facing on torch entwined by serpent.

Tetradrachms.

796. AR ↑ 12.17. Bellinger 371.1.
797. AR ↑ 11.16. Bellinger 370.1.

Obv. IMPCOP...NVS Draped bust of Macrinus r., laureate.
Rev. COL PFL/AVFC/CAESA Founder ploughing r.

798. Æ ↓ 10.43. Kadman 75.

Obv. IMP CA MA.... Bust as above, but seen from the rear.
Rev. ...AVF Tetrastyle temple; within, Tyche standing l., holding bust and scepter.

799. Æ ↑ 12.17.

Diadumenian (A.D. 218)

Obv. MOΠANTΩNINOCKAI Draped bust of Diadumenian r.
Rev. ΔHMAPXEΞOYCIAC Eagle, head l., standing facing on torch entwined by serpent; between legs, bull's head r.

Tetradrachm.

800. AR ↑ 12.01. Khirbet el Atmaniyeh hoard of 1937. Bellinger 373.1.

Obv. MOP·DIADVMENIANVS.... Draped bust of Diadumenian r.
Rev. COLIFLAV ... CAES Bust of Sarapis r.

801. Æ ↑ 7.92. A. Cahn sale 71, 14 Oct. 1931, 1088.

Elagabalus (A.D. 218–22)

Obv. IMPMAVAN TONINVS Draped bust of Elagabalus r., laureate.
Rev. COLPFA...CAESAR/SPQR in wreath supported by eagle.

802. Æ ↑ 16.01. Kadman 85.
803. Æ ↑ 4.18. Half denomination of 802.
804. Æ ↓ 4.59. As 803, but crude style.

Rev. [CIFAVG CAESMETR] Tetrastyle temple; within, Tyche standing l., holding bust and scepter, r. foot on harbor god.

805. Æ ↑ 5.48.

Alexander Severus (A.D. 222–35)

Obv. Laureate head of A. Severus r. (806, 808–16) or draped bust r., laureate (807).
Rev. Inscription within wreath (806) or SPQR within wreath supported by eagle (807–16).

806. Æ ↑ 12.90. *Obv.* IMPC SEV ALEXAND *Rev.* COL / IFAVFC / CAESAR / METRO / POLI.
807. Æ ↑ 10.61. *Obv.* IMCAESALEXANDER *Rev.* CIFAFC CAEMETROPOLI.
808. Æ ↑ 9.86. Lead "wound." Inscriptions as 807.
809. Æ ↑ 12.95. *Obv.* IMPCAE SEVALVXAND [*sic*]. *Rev.* CPFA-FCCAESMETROPOLI.

The letter C on most coins like nos. 808–9 is written G. This additional stroke has led others to believe that there is the letter I after C.

810. Æ ↓ 10.96. Lead "wound." *Obv.* IMCSEVEAL EXANDER *Rev.* CSFAF Khirbet el Atmaniyeh hoard of 1937.
811. Æ ↓ 6.40. *Obv.* IMPALE *Rev.* CLFA.
812. Æ ↓ 7.37. *Obv.* IMP...EXANDER *Rev.* CIFAVFCCAES....
813. Æ ↓ 6.47. *Obv.* IMPALEXAND *Rev.* METROPOL.
814. Æ ↓ 5.42. Lead "wound." *Obv.* ...EXAND *Rev.* COLPFA.
815. Æ ↑ 3.85. *Obv.* ...PESPV.... *Rev.* illegible.
816. Æ ↑ 3.37.

Philip I (A.D. 244–49)

Obv. Laureate head of Philip I r.
Rev. In exergue, ...METR Dionysus reclining l. on panther advancing r.

817. Æ ↓ 19.56. *Obv.* ...PHIL....

Rev. FCCAES.... Emperor standing r., sacrificing before Roma seated l.

818. Æ ↓ 20.12. *Obv.* ...IVLPHILIPPVSAV.

Trajan Decius (A.D. 249–51)

Obv. Draped bust of T. Decius, radiate (819–20, 822–23, 825) or laureate (821, 824, 826–32).
Rev. COLPRFAVGFCCAESMETSP Tyche standing l., holding bust and scepter; to lower r., harbor god holding anchor.

819. Æ ↑ 20.32. *Obv.* IMPCCMESQTRADECIVSPF.... Kadman, 123 (rev. only).

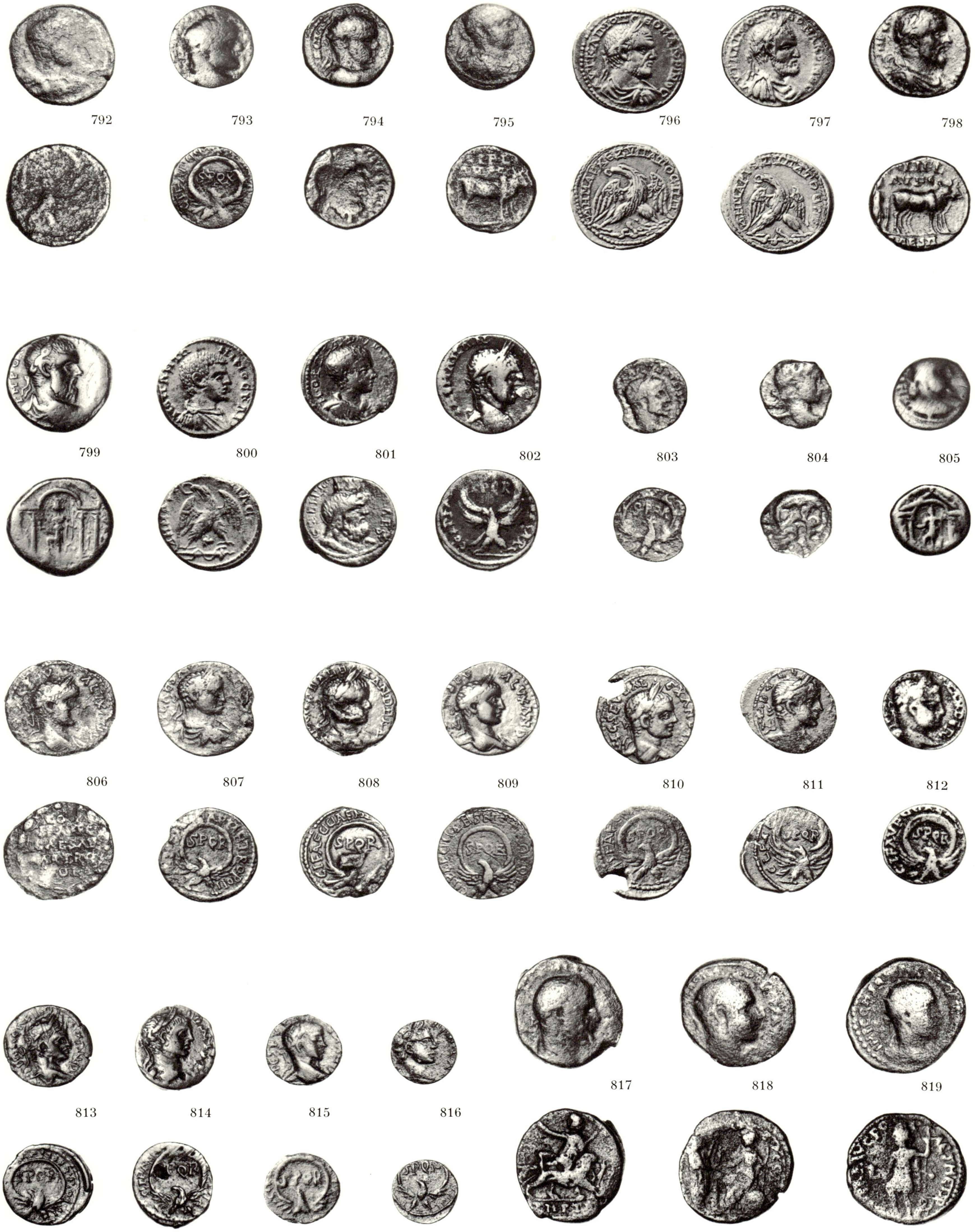

792 793 794 795 796 797 798

799 800 801 802 803 804 805

806 807 808 809 810 811 812

813 814 815 816 817 818 819

820 821 822 823 824 825 826

827 828 829 830 831 832

833 834 835 836 837 838

839 840 841 842 843 844 845

PROVINCIAL CITY COINS: CAESAREA

Trajan Decius (cont.)

Rev. ...CAESMETRO Bust of Tyche r.

820. Æ ↓ 8.62. *Obv.* IMPCMQTRAIANODECIVSAVG.
821. Æ ↓ 5.53. *Obv.* IMPCCMES Rev. COLPFAV.

Rev. ...LPFAVG Eagle supporting bust of Tyche within circle.

822. Æ ↑ 18.38. *Obv.* ....QTRADEC....
823. Æ ↑ 19.08. *Obv.* as 822.

Rev. Inscription as 819. Apollo standing l., holding branch and resting on tripod entwined by serpent.

824. Æ ↓ 17.68. *Obv.* IMPCCMESQTRADECIVSAVG.

Rev. ...AVGFCCAESME.... Roma-Nikephora enthroned l., holding small Nike and scepter.

825. Æ ↑ 16.88. *Obv.* as 824.

Rev. Nike standing r. and emperor standing l., facing each other. In exergue, SP.

826. Æ ↑ 18.83. *Obv.* IMPCCMESQTRAIDECIVSAVG *Rev.* COLPRFAVG...ESMETRO Kadman 148 (obv. only; the rev. is of another coin not at ANS).
827. Æ ↑ 16.10. *Obv.* inscription as 826. *Rev.* ...PRFAVGFCCAESMETROPO.

Rev. COLPRFAVGFC.... Vexillum between two eagles.

828. Æ ↑ 19.55. *Obv.* as 824. Probably die of 826. *Rev.* in exergue, METR.

Rev. COLPRFAVGFCCAESMETROP Altar; behind, palm tree and olive tree.

829. Æ ↑ 17.59. *Obv.* inscription as 824.
830. Æ ↑ 13.33. *Obv.* inscription as 824. Worn.

Rev. COLPRFAVGF.... Emperor on horseback r.

831. Æ ↑ 15.93. *Obv.* IMPCCMESQTRA.

Rev. ...PRFAVGFCCAESME.... Poseidon, nude, standing l., holding dolphin and trident.

832. Æ ↑ 18.21. *Obv.* ...ECIVSAVG.

Herennia Etruscilla

Obv. Draped bust of H. Etruscilla r.
Rev. COLPFAVFCCAESMETROP Bust of Tyche r. (833) or l. (834).

833. Æ ↑ 7.81. *Obv.* ERENNIAETRVSCILLAAV.
834. Æ ↑ 7.81. *Obv.* EREN...SCILLAAV.

Rev. CLPFLAVGFCCA...ETSP Cista Mystica on base in middle of four torches.

835. Æ ↑ 17.65. *Obv.* as 833. Kadman 171.

Rev. COLPRFAVFCCAESMETROPO Dionysus standing l., holding thyrsus; in lower l., panther.

836. Æ ↑ 17.00. *Obv.* HERE....

Rev. COLPRFAVG...METRO Tyche standing l., holding bust and scepter; in lower r., harbor god.

837. Æ ↓ 20.90. *Obv.* as 833.

Herennius Etruscus (A.D. 249–51)

Obv. Draped bust of H. Etruscus r., radiate.
Rev. Bust of Tyche r.

838. Æ ↓ 8.50. *Obv.* MESQERENETRVSCODECIOCAES *Rev.* ...ARSMETROPO Kadman 173.
839. Æ ↑ 7.13. *Obv.* MESQERENETRVSDECIOCAES *Rev.* ...AVGCCAESMETROP Kadman 174.
840. Æ ↑ 5.96. *Obv.* MESQERENETRVSD Probably die of 839. *Rev.* COLPFAVGCCAESMETRO.
841. Æ ↓ 5.99. As 840.

Rev. ...CAESM.... Cista Mystica on base in middle of four torches.

842. Æ ↓ 14.23. *Obv.* inscription illegible. Kadman 184.

Rev. ...CAE/METSP Vexillum between two addorsed eagles.

843. Æ ↓ 19.16. *Obv.* inscription illegible.

Hostilian (A.D. 251)

Obv. HOSTILIANOQVINTOC Draped bust of Hostilian r., laureate (844, 846–47, 849) or radiate (845, 848).
Rev. COLPFAVFCCAESMETROP Bust of Tyche r. (844–45) or l. (846–48).

844. Æ ↓ 8.47. Kadman 188.
845. Æ ↓ 5.75. *Obv.* HOSTILIANOQVI.... *Rev.* COLPFAVF[CCAES] METROP.

PROVINCIAL CITY COINS: CAESAREA

Hostilian (cont.)

846. Æ ↓ 8.41.
847. Æ ↓ 6.15. Kadman 190.
848. Æ ↓ 7.09. *Obv.* HOSTILIAN .... *Rev.* ...FCCAESMET Kadman 174. (rev. only, and wrongly attributed to H. Etruscus. See 839 above).

Rev. COLPFAVFC...ROP Sarapis standing facing, looking l., with r. arm raised, holding scepter in l.

849. Æ ↓ 6.81. *Obv.* HOSTILIANVDQVINT....

Trebonianus Gallus (A.D. 251–53)

Obv. Draped bust of T. Gallus r., laureate (850–51) or radiate (852).
Rev. COLPFAVGFCCAESMETROP Tyche standing l., holding bust and scepter; in lower r., harbor god.

850. Æ ↓ 10.28. *Obv.* ...VIBGALLVSPFAVG.

Rev. ...OLPFAVGFCCAESMETROP Vexillum between two addorsed eagles; in exergue, PSPA.

851. Æ ↓ 12.68. *Obv.* IMPCCVIBGALLVSPFAVG.

Rev. COLPFAVGFCCAES.... Eagle supporting bust of Tyche within wreath.

852. Æ ↑ 13.11. *Obv.* as 851.

Volusian (A.D. 251–53)

Obv. IMPCCVOLVSIANVSPFAVG Draped bust of Volusian r., laureate (853, 856–57) or radiate (854–55).
Rev. ...FAVFCCAESMETR Bust of Tyche r.

853. Æ ↑ 7.80. Kadman 218.

Rev. COLPFAVGFCCAESMETPRSPAL Emperor on horseback r.

854. Æ ↓ 14.22.
855. Æ ↑ 13.71.

Rev. ...CAESMET.... Dionysus reclining l., on panther advancing r.; in exergue: SPAL.

856. Æ ↑ 11.46. *Obv.* IMPCCVOLVSI.
857. Æ ↑ 10.90. *Obv.* inscription as 856.

CAESAREA PANIAS

Local era beginning 3 B.C.

Time of Nero

Obv. DIVA POPPAEAAV Distyle temple; within, female figure seated l., holding cornucopiae.
Rev. DIVA C[LAVD]NERF Round hexastyle temple; within, female figure standing l., holding cornucopiae. A.D. 63/4. (See M. Grant, "The Patterns of Official Coinage...," *Essays Mattingly*, p. 98.)

858. Æ ↑ 6.06. Naville 11, 18 June 1925, 415. Found east of the Jordan.

Time of Marcus Aurelius

Obv. Inscription illegible. Head of Tyche r.
Rev. KAICAP / ΠΑΝΙΑ / ΔΟC Above, BOP (A.D. 169), all within wreath.

859. Æ ↑ 8.88.

Obv. Inscription illegible. Head of Pan r.
Rev. ΚΑΙϹΑΡ·ΠΑΝΙΑ ΔΟϹ·ΡΟΒ· (A.D. 169). Syrinx.

860. Æ ↑ 3.17.

Marcus Aurelius (A.D. 161–80)

Obv. Draped bust of M. Aurelius r., laureate.
Rev. ΚΑΙϹΕΒΙΕΡΚΑΙΑϹΥΤΠΠΑΝΕΙΩ Zeus, nude, standing l., holding patera and scepter; to r., ΡΟΒ (A.D. 169).

861. Æ ↑ 11.04. *Obv.* ΑΥΤΚΑΙϹΜΑΥΡΑΝΤΩΝΙΝ.

Rev. ΚΑΙϹΕΒΙΕΡΚΑΙΑϹΥΤΠΠΑΝΕΙΩ Pan standing facing, leaning r. against tree trunk, playing flute; to l. and r., ΡΟ Β (A.D. 169).

862. Æ ↑ 12.20. *Obv.* ΑΥΤΚΑΙϹΜΑΥΡΑΝΤΩΝΕΙ.
863. Æ ↑ 13.79. As 862.

Commodus (A.D. 177–92)

Obv. ΑΥΚ·Μ·ΑΥΡ·ΑΝΤΟΚΟΜ Laureate head of Commodus r.
Rev. ΚΑΙϹϹΕΒΙΕΡΚΑΙ ΑϹΥΤΠΠΑΝΕΙΩ Pan standing facing, leaning r. against tree trunk, playing flute; to l. and r., ΡϞ Α (A.D. 188).

864. Æ ↑ 9.29.

Septimius Severus (A.D. 193–211)

Obv. Laureate head of S. Severus r.
Rev. ΚΑΙϹЄΒΙЄΡΚΑΙΑϹΥΤΠΑΝΕΙ Pan standing facing, leaning r. against tree trunk, playing flute; to l. and r., ΘΡ Ϟ [*sic*] (A.D. 196).

865. Æ ↑ 8.80. *Obv.* ΑΥΤ.Λ.ϹЄΠϹЄΥ....

Rev. ΚΑΙϹЄΒΙЄΡΚΑΙΑϹΥΛΤΠΑ[ΝΕΙΩ] Tyche standing r., resting l. foot on rock, holding rudder and cornucopiae; to l. and r., ΡϞ Θ (A.D. 196).

866. Æ ↑ 11.32. *Obv.* inscription as 865.

Julia Domna

Obv. Draped bust of J. Domna r.
Rev. ΚΑΙϹЄΒΙЄΡΚΑΙΑϹΥΛΤΠΑΝΕΙ Tyche standing facing, looking r., holding rudder and cornucopiae; to l. and r., C B (A.D. 199).

867. Æ ↑ 11.21. *Obv.* ΙΟΥΛΙΑ....

Rev. Inscription as 867. Syrinx and pedum; above, CB (A.D. 199).

868. Æ ↑ 4.83. *Obv.* ΙΟΥΛΙΑ...ΜΝΑϹЄΒ.
869. Æ ↑ 4.56. As 868, but syrinx and pedum reversed.

Caracalla (A.D. 198–217)

Obv. Draped bust of young Caracalla r., laureate (870–71) or laureate head r. (872–73).
Rev. ΚΑΙϹΕΒΙΕΡ. . . ΝΙ Pan standing facing, leaning r. against tree trunk, playing flute; to. l. and r., ΘϞ Ψ (A.D. 196).

870. Æ ↑ 8.85. *Obv.* ΑΥΤΚΑΙϹΜΑΥΡΑΝΤΩΝΙ.
871. Æ ↑ 9.14. *Obv.* ΑΥΤΚΑΙ...ΑΝΤΩΝ *Rev.* Κ ΙϹΕΒΙΕΡ ΤΠΑ.

1201 1202 1203 1204 1205 1206

1207 1208 1209 1210 1211 1212

1213 1214 1215 1216

1217

1218 1219 1220 1221 1222 1223 1224

1225

1226

1227

1228

1229 1230 1231 1232 1233 1234 1235 1236 1237 1238 1239 1240 1241 1242 1243 1244 1245 1246 1247 1248 1249 1250 1251 1252 1253 1254 1255 1256

DECAPOLIS, ETC.: BOSTRA (cont.)

Julia Mamaea

Obv. IVLIAMAMAEAAVGVSTA Draped bust of J. Mamaea r.
Rev. N·TR·ALEXANDRI ANAE / COL·BOSTR Tetrastyle temple; within, Tyche standing facing, holding scepter surmounted by small trophy; resting l. foot on river god; to l. and r., centaur.

1229. Æ ↓ 14.33.
1230. Æ ↓ 14.48.

Rev. COLONIA BO STRA Type as 1218.

1231. Æ ↓ 6.01.
1232. AR ↓ 6.51.
1233. Æ ↓ 5.64. Probably dies of 1232.
1234. Æ ↓ 8.20. *Obv.* die of 1232.
1235. Æ ↓ 7.78. *Obv.* die of 1232.
1236. Æ ↓ 6.22.

Rev. COLONIA BOSTRA Type as 1222.

1237. Æ ↓ 4.08.
1238. Æ ↓ 4.19.
1239. Æ ↓ 5.20.
1240. Æ ↓ 6.16.

Rev. Inscription as 1229. Type as 1227.

1241. Æ ↓ 4.40.

Philip I (A.D. 244–49)

Obv. IMPCASMIVL PHILIPPOSAVG Laureate bust of Philip I r., draped.
Rev. COLMETROPOLIS BOSTRA Laureate bust of Dusares r., draped.

1242. Æ ↗ 19.23.

Rev. COLMETRO POLIS BOSTRA Bust of Zeus-Ammon r. wearing kalathos.

1243. Æ ↓ 17.38.
1244. Æ ↙ 16.64. *Rev.* die of 1243.
1245. Æ ↑ 15.28.

Philip II (A.D. 247–49)

Obv. MARCIVLPHILIPPOSCESAR Draped bust of Philip II (1246), radiate (1247–50).
Rev. COLMETROPOLIS BOSTRA AKTI/AΔOVC/APIA (1246) or AKTI/AΔOV/CAPIA within agonistic wreath.

1246. Æ ↓ 19.51.
1247. Æ ↑ 18.18.
1248. Æ ↓ 19.69. *Obv.* die of 1247.
1249. Æ ↑ 13.06.
1250. Æ ↑ 13.75.

Trajan Decius (A.D. 249–51)

Obv. Inscription illegible. Laureate bust of T. Decius r.
Rev. CONCORDIAE BOSTRENRVM Zeus Ammon (l.) and Tyche (r.) standing, clasping hands.

1251. Æ ↑ 12.68. Worn and corroded.

Herennia Etruscilla

Obv. ERENNIAETRVSCILLAAVG Draped bust of H. Etruscilla r.
Rev. ACTIADVSA...BOSTRA Stepped altar, upon which baetyl surmounted by seven flat objects; flanked by two small baetyls; all within wreath.

1252. Æ ↓ 12.65.
1253. Æ ↑ 13.65. *Obv.* die of 1252.

Rev. ...ETROPOLBO.... Zeus-Ammon standing l., holding uncertain object and spear surmounted by trophy; at his feet to l., small figure of ram.

1254. Æ ↑ 8.34.

Herennius Etruscus and Hostilian (A.D. 251)

Obv. VALENSCVINTVSCAI Confronted busts of H. Etruscus and Hostilian.
Rev. ...IABOSTRENRVM Zeus-Ammon (l.) and Tyche (r.) standing, clasping hands.

1255. Æ ↓ 12.80.
1256. Æ ↑ 12.79.

DECAPOLIS, ETC.: CANATA

Local (Pompeian) era beginning 64/3 B.C..

Claudius (A.D. 41–54)

Obv. Inscription illegible. Laureate head of Claudius l.
Rev. ΚΑΝΑΤΗΝΩΝ Veiled head of Tyche l.

1257. Æ ↑ 5.86. Worn. *Rev.* downward to r., ΒΙΡ (A.D. 48).
1258. Æ ↑ 5.66. Very worn. *Rev.* date off flan.

Domitian (A.D. 81–96)

Obv. ΔΟΜΙΤΙ ΚΑΙCΑ.... Laureate bust of Domitian l.
Rev. ΚΑΝΑΤ Bust of Tyche l.

1259. Æ ↑ 2.72.
1260. Æ ↑ 2.03.
1261. Æ ↑ 2.49.
1262. Æ ↑ 3.17.
1263. Æ ↑ 2.58.

Commodus (A.D. 177–92)

Obv. ΑVΤΚΜΑV ΑΝΤΟΚΟΜ Laureate bust, draped (1264, 1267–69) or laureate head (1265–66) of Commodus r.
Rev. ΓΑΒΕΙΝ Є ΚΑΝΑ ΘΙΗΝ [*sic*]. Tyche standing l., wearing short chiton, holding small figure of Nike and cornucopiae; to l. and r. ΓΝ C (A.D. 190).

1264. Æ ↑ 12.04.

Rev. ΓΑΒЄΙΝ ΚΑΝΑΘ Dionysus, half-draped, standing facing, looking l., holding oinochoe and thyrsus; to l., panther seated l.; downward to r., ΓΝC (A.D. 190).

1265. Æ ↑ 6.86.
1266. Æ ↑ 8.25. *Obv.* die of 1265.

Rev. ΓΑΝ...ΑΝΑ.... Bust of Athena r., wearing crested helmet.

1267. Æ ↑ 2.60. *Obv.* ΚΟΜΟ ΑΝΤΟΝΟC.
1268. Æ ↓ 2.44. *Obv.* ΚΟΜ...ΑΝΤΟΝΟ *Rev.* ΓΑ ΚΑΝΑΘ.
1269. Æ ↑ 2.50. *Obv.* ...ΝΤΟΝΟC *Rev.* ΓΑΒ ΚΑΝΑ.

CAPITOLIAS

Local era beginning A.D. 97/8

Marcus Aurelius (A.D. 161–80)

Obv. ΑVΤΚΑΙCΜΑVΡ ΑΝΤѠΝЄΙΝΟC Draped bust of M. Aurelius r.
Rev. ΚΑΠΙΤѠ ΛΙΕѠΝ ΙΑΑ Hexastyle temple; within, Tyche standing l., holding small bust and scepter; resting r. foot on river god; to l., ·Ο· (A.D. 167).

1270. Æ ↑ 10.81.
1271. Æ ↑ 10.96. *Obv.* die of 1270.
1272. Æ ↑ 9.55.

Rev. ΚΑΠΙΤѠΛΙΕ ѠΝΙΕΡ ΑCVΑVΤ Tetrastyle temple, flanked by two towers; within, Zeus seated l., holding scepter; above, propylon; date off flan, possibly Θ Ξ (A.D. 166), see *Syria* 36 (1959), p. 76, no. 6, and Sp. l.

1273. Æ ↑ 19.04.

Commodus (A.D. 177–92)

Obv. [ΑVΤΚΜΑV]Ρ Κ[ΟΜΟΔΟC] Laureate bust of Commodus r.
Rev. ΚΑΠΙΑΛΕ ΞΜΑ ΚΕΓΕΝ Youthful male bust r., draped (Alexander the Great?); to l. and r., Γ Ϥ (A.D.190).

1274. Æ ↑ 9.13.

Macrinus (A.D. 217–18)

Obv. ...ΑV...ΙΝΟCCЄ Laureate bust of Macrinus r., draped.
Rev. ΚΑΠΙΤѠ ΑC ΑV Octastyle temple; within, Zeus seated l., holding eagle (?) and scepter; above, propylon and date, off flan, Ρ Κ (A.D. 217).

1275. Æ ↑ 23.34. *Syria* 36 (1959), p. 77, no. 13, pl. 12 and Sp. 21 (this coin).

Elagabalus (A.D. 218–22)

Obv. ΑVΚΜΑ ΑΝΤѠΝΙ Laureate bust of Elagabalus r., cuirassed.
Rev. Octastyle temple; within, Zeus seated l., holding eagle (?) and scepter; above, propylon and [Ρ] ΚΒ (A.D. 219).

1276. Æ ↑ 11.22. *Syria* 36 (1959), p. 77, no. 14c, pl. 12 (this coin).

DIUM

Local (Pompeian) era beginning 64/3 B.C.

Caracalla (A.D. 198–217)

Obv. Laureate bust of Caracalla, draped.
Rev. ΔЄΙΗΝ ѠΝ ΚΟΙ CV Hexastyle temple; within, flaming altar; in pediment, flying eagle.

1277. Æ ↑ 14.07. *Obv.* ΑΚ·Μ·ΑV ΑΝΤѠΝЄΙΝ *Rev.* downward to l., ΗΞC (A.D. 206).
1278. Æ ↑ 14.21. *Obv.* ΑVΤΚΜΑΝΤѠCЄ *Rev.* ΔЄΙΗΝ ѠΝ ΚΟΙC. To l. and r. above, Ο C (A.D. 207). *Syria* 36 (1959), p. 77, no. 16, pl. 13, 15 (this coin).

1279. Æ ↑ 15.05. Dies of 1278.
1280. Æ ↑ 12.41. *Obv.* ΑVΚΜΑV ΑΝΤѠΝ CЄ *Rev.* ΔЄΙΗΝ ѠΝ ΚΟΙCV Downward to l., ΑΟC (A.D. 208).

Geta (A.D. 209–12)

Obv. ΠΟVΠ C ΓЄΤΑCΚ Bust of Geta r.
Rev. ΔЄΙΗΝ ѠΝ Zeus-Heliopolites (Hadad) standing facing, holding scepter surmounted by eagle and small Nike extending wreath; at his feet to l. and r., forepart of recumbent bull; downward to l., ΗΞC (A.D. 206).

1281. Æ ↑ 10.91.
1282. Æ ↑ 13.81.

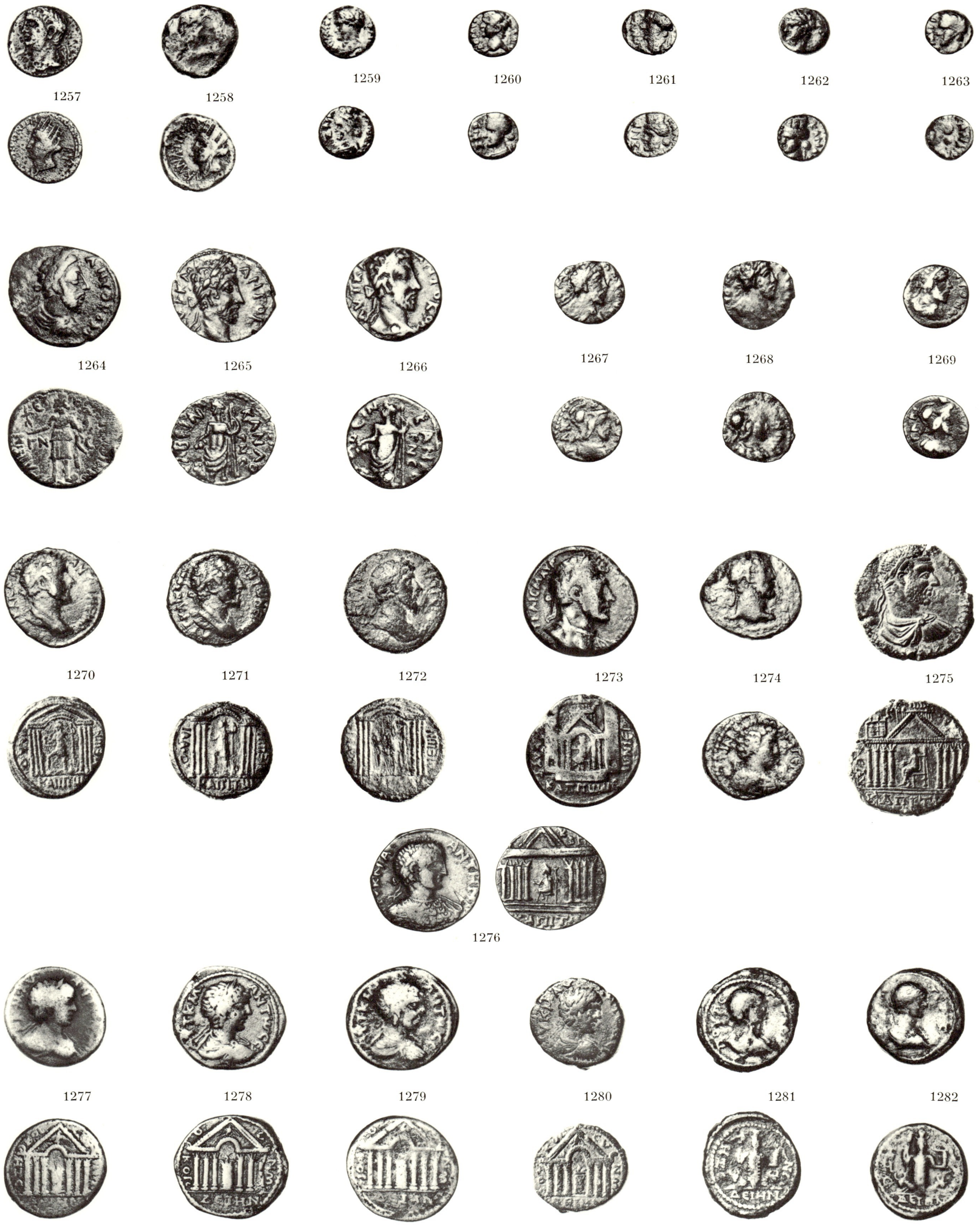

1257 1258 1259 1260 1261 1262 1263

1264 1265 1266 1267 1268 1269

1270 1271 1272 1273 1274 1275

1276

1277 1278 1279 1280 1281 1282

1283

1284

1285

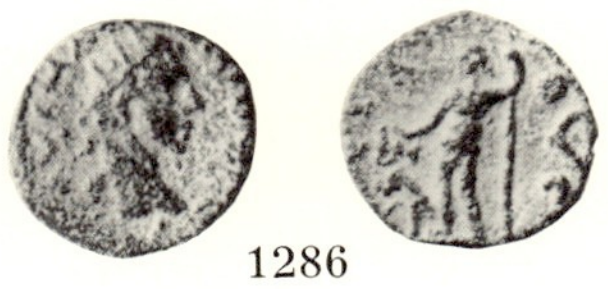
1286

1287

1288

1289

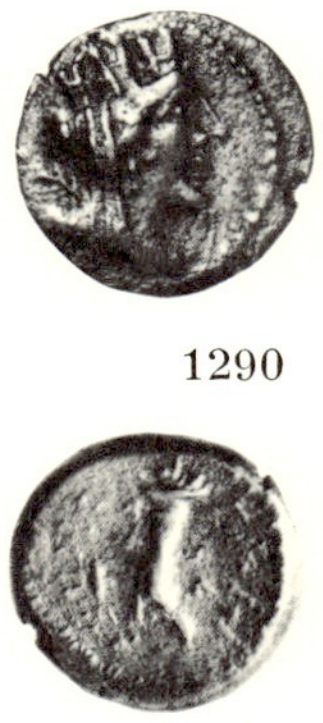
1290

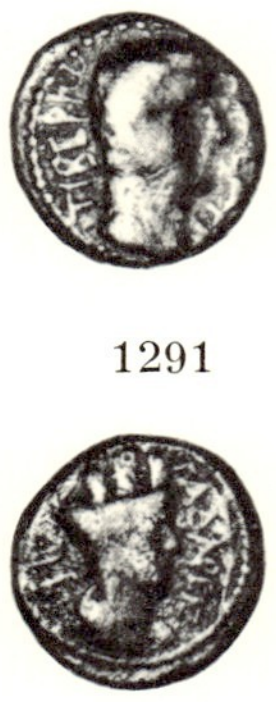
1291

1292

1293

1294

1295

1296

1297

1298

1299

1300

1301

1302

1303

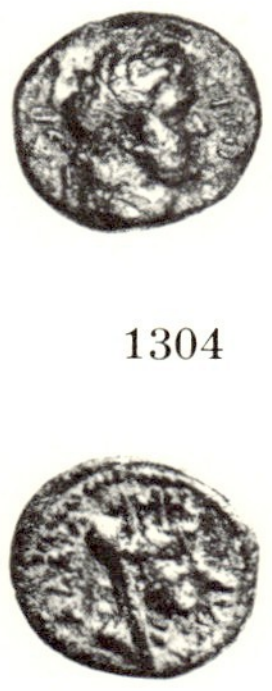
1304

1305

1306

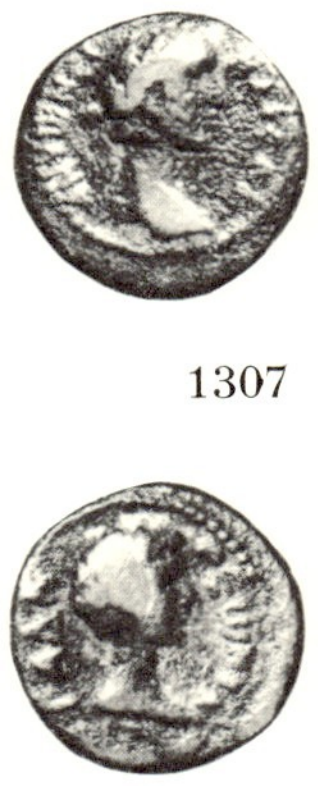
1307

1308

1309

1310

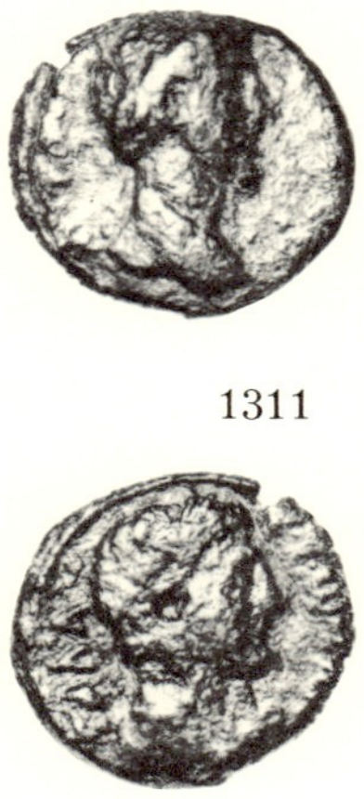
1311

DECAPOLIS, ETC.: ESBUS

Elagabalus (A.D. 218–22)

Obv. Draped bust of Elagabalus, radiate (1283–84, 1286), or laureate (1285).
Rev. [AVPЄCB]OVC Zeus seated l., holding phiale and scepter.

1283. Æ ↓ 14.54. *Obv.* ...ANT....
1284. Æ ↓ 8.18. (Smaller denomination?) *Obv.* inscription as 1283.

Rev. AVPЄCB OVC Mên standing l., holding small round object and scepter entwined by serpent.

1285. Æ ↑ 7.73. *Obv.* AVTCMAVPANTONINVS.

Rev. AVPЄCB OVC Dionysus, nude, standing l., pouring wine from oinochoe and holding thyrsus; at his feet to l., panther.

1286. Æ ↓ 5.63. *Obv.* AVKM...NTONINV.

GADARA

Local (Pompeian) era beginning 64/3 B.C.

Pseudo-Autonomous

Obv. Veiled bust of Tyche r.; behind shoulder, palm branch.
Rev. ΓΑΔΑ ΡΕѠΝ Cornucopiae.

1287. Æ ↖ 5.28. *Rev.* upward to l., LIH (47/6 B.C.).
1288. Æ ↑ 2.87. *Rev.* downward to l., LEK (40/39 B.C.).
1289. Æ ↑ 3.29. *Rev.* downward to l., LK[Ϛ?] (39/8? B.C.).
1290. Æ ↑ 4.59. *Rev.* date illegible.

Tiberius (A.D. 14–37)

Obv. TIBЄPIѠ KAICAPI Head of Tiberius r.
Rev. ΓΑΔΑΡΕΙϹ Veiled bust of Tyche r.; upward to r., LϤB (A.D. 29/30).

1291. Æ ↑ 5.12.
1292. Æ ↑ 6.13.
1293. Æ ↑ 5.34.

Claudius (A.D. 41–54)

Obv. CЄBACTOC Laureate bust of Claudius r.
Rev. ΓΑΔΑ Veiled bust of Tyche r.; in lower r., LHP (A.D. 44/5).

1294. Æ ↑ 4.66.
1295. Æ ↑ 4.10. Probably rev. die of 1294.
1296. Æ ↑ 4.47.

Rev. ΓΑΔΑΡΑ Two cornucopiae crossed; above, ΔIP (A.D. 50/1).

1297. Æ ↑ 1.82.

Nero (A.D. 54–67)

Obv. Laureate bust (1298) or head (1299) of Nero r.
Rev. ΓΑΔΑΡΕΩΝ Two cornucopiae crossed; above, LAΛP (A.D. 67/8).

1298. Æ ↑ 5.02. *Obv.* ΝΕΡΩΝ.

Rev. ΓΑΔΑΡΑ Tyche standing l., holding wreath and cornucopiae; in lower l., palm branch; to l., LAΛP (A.D. 67/8).

1299. Æ ↑ 9.89. *Obv.* ΝΕΡΩΝΙΚ...ϹΑΡ.

Vespasian (A.D. 69–79)

Obv. ...OCKAICAPOYЄCΠ.... Laureate bust of Vespasian r.; countermark over ear: head.
Rev. ΓΑΔΑΡ Tyche standing l., holding wreath and cornucopiae; in lower l., palm branch; to l., LЄΛP (A.D. 71/2).

1300. Æ ↑ 10.84.
1301. Æ ↑ 11.08.

Titus (A.D. 79–81)

Obv. TITOC...AP Laureate bust of Titus r.
Rev. ΓΑΔΑΡΕΩΝ Two cornucopiae crossed; above, LZΛP (A.D. 73).

1302. Æ ↑ 5.41.
1303. Æ ↑ 5.20.

Rev. ΓΑΔΑΡΑ Veiled bust of Tyche r.; upward to r., LZΛP (A.D. 73/4).

1304. Æ ↑ 3.09.

Antoninus Pius (A.D. 138–61)

Obv. Bust of Antoninus Pius r., laureate and draped (1305–6), or laureate (1307).
Rev. ΠΟΓΑΔΑΡ/Ι·Α·Α·Γ·/Κ·CY Tetrastyle temple; within, Zeus seated three-quarters facing, holding Nike and scepter; in pediment, ΓKC (A.D. 159/60).

1305. Æ ↑ 22.82. *Obv.* AVTKAICANTѠ NЄINOCCЄBCYC.

Rev. ΓΑΔΑΡΕѠΝ Tyche standing l., holding scepter and cornucopiae; to r., column surmounted by small Nike extending wreath; below, river god; upward to r., ΓKC (A.D. 159/60).

1306. Æ ↑ 9.51. *Obv.* KAICAP CЄB.

Rev. ΓΑΔΑΡЄѠΝ Youthful bust of Heracles r.; downward in lower r., ΓKC (A.D. 159/60).

1307. Æ ↑ 7.27. *Obv.* ANTѠNЄI KAICAP.

Marcus Aurelius (A.D. 161–80)

Obv. Bust of M. Aurelius r., laureate and draped (1308–9) or laureate (1310–11).
Rev. ΓΑΔΑΡΕѠΝ Tyche standing r., holding scepter and cornucopiae; resting l. foot on river god; to r., column surmounted by small Nike extending wreath; upward to r., ЄKC (A.D. 161/2).

1308. Æ ↑ 7.35. *Obv.* AYTKAICMAYP ANTѠNЄINOC.

Rev. ΠΟΜΓΑΔΑΡ/ΙΑΑΓ/KCYP Tetrastyle temple; within, Zeus seated three-quarters facing, holding Nike and scepter; in pediment, ϚKC (A.D. 162/3).

1309. Æ ↑ 12.77. *Obv.* inscription as 1308.

Rev. ΓΑΔΑ ΡЄѠΝ Laureate bust of Heracles, draped in lion skin; downward to r., ϚKC(?) (A.D. 162/3?).

1310. Æ ↑ 11.02. *Obv.* ...ANTѠNЄI.
1311. Æ ↑ 9.63. *Obv.* die of 1310.

DECAPOLIS, ETC.: GADARA (cont.)

Faustina I

Obv. CЄBACTH Draped bust of Faustina r.
Rev. ΓΑΔΑΡЄѠΝ Laureate bust of Zeus r., draped; downward in lower r., ЄKC (A.D. 161).

1312. Æ ↑ 6.76.
1313. Æ ↑ 8.13.
1314. Æ ↑ 4.24.

Lucius Verus (A.D. 161–69)

Obv. Laureate bust of L. Verus r.
Rev. ΓΑΔΑΡЄѠΝ Youthful bust of Heracles r.; downward in lower r., ΔKC (A.D. 161).

1315. Æ ↑ 6.59. *Obv.* AVTKAICA AYPOVHPOC.
1316. Æ ↑ 5.48. *Obv.* inscription as 1315.

Rev. ΠΟΜ ΓΑ·ΔΑΡ Laureate bust of Heracles r., draped in lion skin; downward in lower r., ЄKC (A.D. 161/2).

1317. Æ ↑ 12.88.

Commodus (A.D. 177–92)

Obv. AVTKΛAVP KOMMOΔO Laureate bust of Commodus r.
Rev. ΠΟΜ ΓΑΔΑΡЄѠΝ Laureate bust of Heracles, draped in lion skin; downward in lower r. ΓMC (A.D. 179/80).

1318. Æ ↑ 9.87.

Rev. ΓΑΔΑΡ Tyche standing r., holding scepter and cornucopiae; resting l. foot on river god; to r., column surmounted by small Nike extending wreath; upward to r., ЄMC (A.D. 181/2). The letter, Є, in the date is not quite clear and is sometimes interpreted as Γ.

1319. Æ ↑ 8.03.
1320. Æ ↑ 7.19. Probably obv. die of 1319.

Caracalla and Geta

Obv. ...MAVPANTѠN.... Caracalla and Geta standing facing each other, clasping hands.
Rev. ΠΟ ΓΑΔΑ.... Tetrastyle temple; within, Zeus seated facing, holding small Nike and scepter; in pediment, BΞC (A.D. 198/9).

1321. Æ ↑ 16.93.

Caracalla (A.D. 198–217)

Obv. AVTKAIANTѠ NINOCCЄB Laureate bust of Caracalla r., draped.
Rev. ΔHMAPXЄΞ·VΠA·TO·Δ Eagle standing facing with spread wings, looking l., holding wreath in beak; between legs, the three Graces within wreath.

Tetradrachm.

1322. AR ↑ 13.05. Khirbet el Atmaniyeh hoard of 1937. Bellinger 322.

Obv. Type as 1322.
Rev. ΠΟΜ/ΠΗΙЄѠΝ/ΓΑΔΑΡΕ Galley sailing l., row of oarsmen and helmsman; aphlaston at stern; above and below galley, ЄT/HOC (A.D. 214/5).

1323. Æ ↑ 25.17. *Obv.* AVTKM ANTONЄIN.

Rev. ΠΟΜ/ΓΑΔΑΡЄ Tetrastyle temple; within, Zeus seated l., holding small Nike and scepter; in pediment, HOC (A.D. 214/5)

1324. Æ ↑ 11.76. *Obv.* inscription illegible.
1325. Æ ↑ 16.88. *Obv.* inscription illegible.

Rev. ΠΟΜΠΗΙЄѠΝ ΓΑΔΑΡЄѠΝ Laureate head of Heracles, draped in lion skin; date illegible.

1326. Æ ↑ 10.33. *Obv.* AVTKM ANTѠNЄIN·

Macrinus (A.D. 217–18)

Obv. AVTKMOΠCЄ.... Laureate bust of Macrinus r.
Rev. ΔHMAPXЄΞVΠATΠΠ Eagle standing facing with spread wings, looking l., holding wreath in beak; between legs, the three Graces within wreath.

Tetradrachm.

1327. AR ↑ 13.91. Bellinger 327.

Diadumenian (A.D. 218)

Obv. OΠЄΛΛIOC ANTѠNINOCK Draped bust of Diadumenian r.
Rev. ΔHMAPXЄΞVΠATOΠΠ Eagle standing facing with spread wings, looking l., holding wreath in beak; between legs, the three Graces within wreath.

Tetradrachm.

1328. AR ↗ 15.46. Bellinger 336.

Elagabalus (A.D. 218–22)

Obv. Draped bust of Elagabalus r., laureate (1329) or radiate (1330–31).
Rev. ΓΑΔΑΡ ЄѠΝ Heracles, wearing short tunic, standing r., holding uncertain object, reaching for cista mystica to r., surmounting small column; at feet to l., small animal; to r., small lion rearing up against column; downward to l., AΠC (A.D. 218/9).

1329. Æ ↑ 14.52. *Obv.*. ...MAV ANTѠNЄIN.

Rev. ΠΟΜ/ΓΑΔΑΡЄ/ѠΝЄΤ Galley sailing l.; row of oarsmen and captain standing in prow, holding standard; above, AΠC (A.D. 218/9).

1330. Æ ↑ 21.40. *Obv.* AVKMAVPANTѠNINOC.

Rev. ΓΑΔΑ/ΡЄѠΝ The three Graces; above, AΠC (A.D. 218/9).

1331. Æ ↑ 8.91. *Obv.* AVKMAVPANTѠ NIN Bellinger, p. 91, pl. 22, 14.

Gordian III (A.D. 238–44)

Obv. AVTOK·K·MAPANTѠΓΟΡΔΙΑΟΝ (1332–40) or AVTKMAN ΓΟΡΔΙΑΝΟ (1341) Bust of Gordion III r., laureate and draped (1331–37, 1339–40), radiate and cuirassed (1338), or radiate (1341).
Rev. ΠΟΜΠ/ΓΑΔΑΡ/ЄѠΝ Galley sailing r.; row of oarsmen; navigator in stern and captain in prow, holding standard; below, ΓT (A.D. 239/40).

1332. Æ ↖ 10.07.
1333. Æ ↑ 11.84. *Rev.* die of 1332.
1334. Æ ↑ 14.57. *Obv.* die of 1333.
1335. Æ ↖ 11.63.

1312 1313 1314 1315 1316 1317

1318 1319 1320 1321 1322 1323

1324 1325 1326 1327 1328 1329

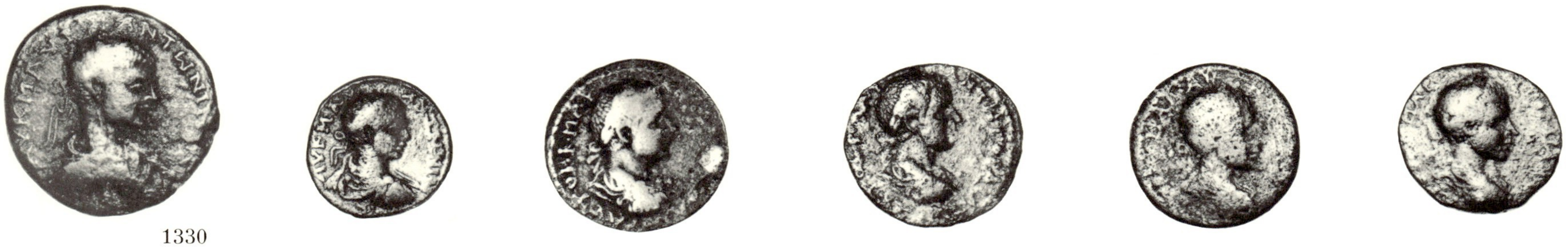

1330 1331 1332 1333 1334 1335

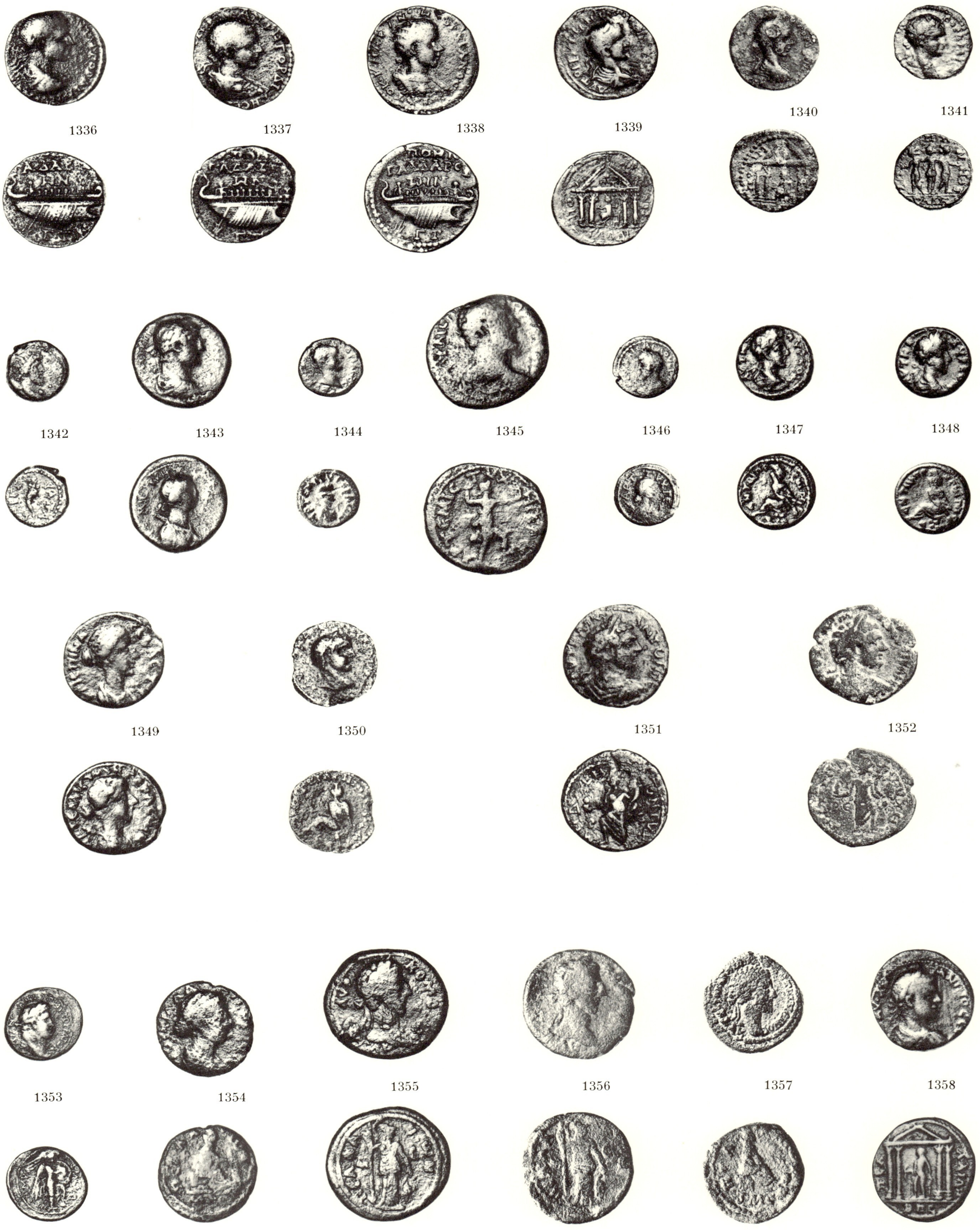

1336 1337 1338 1339 1340 1341

1342 1343 1344 1345 1346 1347 1348

1349 1350 1351 1352

1353 1354 1355 1356 1357 1358

DECAPOLIS, ETC.: GADARA

Gordion III (cont.)

1336. Æ ↖ 10.00.
1337. Æ ↖ 13.66.
1338. Æ ↖ 10.99.

Rev. ΠΟΜ ΓΑΔΑΡ ЄѠΝ Tetrastyle temple; within, Zeus seated l., holding small Nike and scepter; in pediment, ΓΤ (A.D. 239/40).

1339. Æ ↑ 9.45. *Obv.* ΑVΤΟ Κ ΚΑΙΜΑΡ.
1340. Æ ↖ 6.81. *Obv.* ...ΤΟ ΓΟΡΔΙΑΝΟC.

Rev. ΠΟΜΠ ΓΑΔΑΡЄѠΝ The three Graces; above, ΔΤ (A.D. 240/1).

1341. Æ ↑ 6.15. Bellinger, p. 91, pl. 22, 15.

GERASA

Local (Pompeian) era beginning 64/3 B.C.

Quasi-Autonomous

Obv. Diademed bust of Zeus r.
Rev. LΛΡ ΓЄΡΑΣΑ Cornucopiae. A.D. 67/8.

1342. Æ ↑ 4.64.

Hadrian (A.D. 117–38)

Obv. Laureate bust of Hadrian r., draped.
Rev. Draped bust of Artemis-Tyche r.; quiver behind shoulder; to r., bow.

1343. Æ ↑ 11.20. *Obv.* ...ΤΡΑ ΑΔΡΙΑ.... *Rev.* ΑΡΤЄΜΙCΤΥΧΗ ΓЄΡΑ....
1344. Æ ↑ 2.86. *Obv.* CЄΒ ΚΑΙ...ΑΔΡΙΑΝΟC *Rev.* ΑΡΤЄΜΙ-ΤV ΓЄΡΑCѠΝ.

Marcus Aurelius (A.D. 161–80)

Obv. ΑΥΤ ΚΑΙCΜ ΑΥΡΑΝΤѠΝ Laureate bust of M. Aurelius r., draped.
Rev. ΑΡΤЄΜΙC ΤVΧΗ ΓЄΡ Artemis advancing r., drawing arrow from quiver and holding bow; at feet to r., hound running r.

1345. Æ ↑ 13.64.

Lucius Verus (A.D. 161–69)

Obv. ΑVΤΟ Κ ΚΑΙCΑΡ ΛΟVΚΙΟV Laureate bust of L. Verus l.
Rev. ΑΡΤΤVΧ ΓЄ Draped bust of Artemis-Tyche r.; quiver behind shoulder; to r., bow.

1346. Æ ↑ 2.38.

Commodus (A.D. 177–92)

Obv. ΑVΤ ΚΛΑVΡ ΚΟΜ Laureate bust of Commodus r., draped.
Rev. ΑΝΤѠΠΡΧΤѠΠΡ Γ Tyche seated l. on rock, looking back, holding ears of grain; below, half figure of river god.

1347. Æ ↑ 6.82.
1348. Æ ↑ 5.99. *Rev.* die of 1347.

Crispina

Obv. ΚΡΙCΠΙΝΑ CЄΒΑCΤΗ Draped bust of Crispina r.
Rev. ΑΡΤЄΜΙCΤVΧΗ ΓЄΡΑCѠΝ Draped bust of Artemis-Tyche r.; quiver behind shoulder; to r., bow.

1349. Æ ↓ 12.04.

Elagabalus (A.D. 218–22)

Obv. ΑVΤΟ ΚΑΙCΑΡ ΑΝΤѠΝΙ.... Laureate bust of Elagabalus r., draped.
Rev. ΤΥΧΗ ΓЄΡΑCΗΝѠΝ Tyche seated l. on rock, looking back, holding ears of grain; below, half figure of river god; downward to r., ЄΤΑΠC (A.D. 218/9); to l., countermark: bow.

1350. Æ ↑ 9.19.

MEDABA

Local era beginning A.D. 106.

Caracalla (A.D. 198–217)

Obv. ΑVΤ ΚΜΑVΡΑΝΤUΝΙΝV Laureate bust of Caracalla r., draped.
Rev. ΜΗΔΑΒUΝ ΤVΧΗ Tyche standing l., holding small bust and cornucopiae; resting r. foot on prow (?); to l. and r., Ρ Є (A.D. 210/11).

1351. Æ ↓ 9.61.
1352. Æ ↑ 8.53. *Obv.* die of 1351. *Rev.* as 1351, but Tyche standing r., looking l., to l.; ΡЄ (A.D. 210/11).

PELLA

Local (Pompeian) era beginning 64/3 B.C.

Domitian (A.D. 81–96)

Obv. ΑVΤΟ ΚΡΑΤΩΡ ΔΟΜΙΤΙΑΝΟΣ ΚΑΙΣΡ Laureate head of Domitian r.
Rev. ΠΕΛΛΗΝΩΝ Nike standing r., resting l. foot on helmet, writing on shield supported by her l. knee; upward to l., LЄΜΡ (A.D. 82/3).

1353. Æ ↑ 5.26.

Lucilla

Obv. ΛΟV ΚΙΛΛΑ ΑV ΓΟVCΤΑ Draped bust of Lucilla r.
Rev. ΠЄΛΛΑΙѠΝ Tyche seated r. on rock; to r., river god; in exergue, ΜC (A.D. 177/8).

1354. Æ ↑ 8.73.

Commodus (A.D. 177–92)

Obv. ΑV·Κ·ΑVΡ ΚΟΜΟΔΟC Laureate bust of Commodus r.
Rev. ΠЄΛΛΑ Ι·ѠΝ Athena standing facing, looking to r., holding spear and shield; to l. and r. Μ C (A.D. 177/8).

1355. Æ ↑ 16.38.
1356. Æ ↑ 13.89. Probably rev. die of 1355.

Rev. ΠЄΛ ΛΑΙѠΝ Tyche seated r. on rock; to r., river god; in exergue, SΜC (A.D. 183/4).

1357. Æ ↑ 9.83. *Obv.* ΑVΤ ΚΟΜΜΟΔΟC ΑΝΤѠΝЄΙΝΟC.

Elagabalus (A.D. 218–22)

Obv. ΑV·ΑΝ ΤΩΝΙΝΟCCЄ Laureate bust of Elagabalus r., draped.
Rev. ΠЄΛ ΛΑΙΩΝ Tetrastyle temple; within, Apollo standing l., holding bow and branch (?); in exergue, ΒΠC (A.D. 219/20).

1358. Æ ↑ 10.14.

DECAPOLIS, ETC.: PETRA

Quasi-Autonomous

After A.D. 106, the founding of Provincia Arabia.

Obv. Veiled bust of Tyche r.
Rev. Two cornucopiae, crossed.

This unpublished combination of types was struck after A.D. 106, as a continuation of the Nabataean coinage. Later, similar types were struck with the letters ΠΜ in monogram (ΠΕΤΡΑ ΜΗΤΡΟΠΟΛΙC See Sp., p. 220, no. 1.

1359. Æ ↓ 2.26. Bought at Petra in 1967.

Hadrian (A.D. 117–38)

Obv. Laureate bust of Hadrian r., draped and cuirassed.
Rev. ΠΕΤΡΑΜΗΤΡΟΠΟΛΙC (1360–63), often only partially preserved, or ΑΔΡΙΑΝΗΠΕΤΡΑΜΗ-ΤΡΟΠΟΛΙC (1364–65). Tyche seated l. on rock, holding trophy.

1360. Æ ↓ 12.05. *Obv.* ΑV[ΤΟΚΡΑΤωΡ]ΚΑΙCΑΡΤΡΑΙΑΝΟCΑ-ΔΡΙΑΝΟCCЄΒΑCΤΟ.
1361. Æ ↓ 14.20. *Obv.* ΑVΤΟΚΡΑΤωΡΚΑΙCΑΡΤΡΑΙΑΝΟCΑ-ΔΡΙΑΝΟC....
1362. Æ ↓ 13.21. *Obv.* ΑVΤΟΚΡΑΤωΡΚΑΙCΑΡΤΡΑΙΑΝΟCΑ-ΔΡΙΑΝΟCCЄΒΑCΤΟC.
1363. Æ ↓ 12.12. *Obv.* ΑVΤΟΚΡΑΤωΡΚΑΙCΑΡΤΡΑΙΑΝΟC....
1364. Æ ↓ 12.16. *Obv.* inscription as 1362.
1365. Æ ↓ 14.16. *Obv.* inscription as 1362.

Rev. ΑΔΡΙΑΝΗΠΕΤΡΑΜΗΤΡΟΠΟΛΙC Veiled bust of Tyche r.

1366. Æ ↓ 6.46. *Obv.* inscription as 1362.

Marcus Aurelius and Lucius Verus (A.D. 161–69)

Obv. ΑVΤΑΝΤωΝΙΝΟCΚΑΙΟVΗΡΟCCЄΒ Busts of M. Aurelius and L. Verus, confronted.
Rev. ΑΔΠΕΤΡΑΜΗΤΡΟΠΟΛΙC Veiled bust of Tyche r.

1367. Æ ↓ 6.20.

Commodus (A.D. 177–92)

Obv. ΑVΤΚΟΜΜΟ...ΑΝΤ.... Laureate bust of Commodus r.
Rev. ΠΕΤΡΑ/ΜΗΤΡΟ/ΠΟΛΙC within laurel wreath.

1368. Æ ↑ 3.17.

Septimius Severus (A.D. 193–211)

Obv. ...CЄ.... Laureate bust of S. Severus r., draped.
Rev. ΑΔ...ΜΗΤ.... Distyle temple; within, Tyche seated l., holding stele (?) and trophy.

1369. Æ ↑ 5.91.

Caracalla (A.D. 198–217)

Obv. Bust of Caracalla r., laureate (1370–71) and draped (1372).
Rev. Distyle temple; within, Tyche seated l., holding stele (?) and trophy.

1370. Æ ↑ 14.53. *Obv.* ΑVΤ ΜΑΡ ΑΝΤω *Rev.* ΑΔΡ ΠΕΤΡ.
1371. Æ ↑ 13.30. Inscriptions as 1370. *Obv.* to l., countermark: emperor's head; to r., countermark: Є.
1372. Æ ↑ 7.02. *Obv.* ...ΤΚΑΙΜ ΑΝΤΟΝΙΝΟ.... *Rev.* ΠΕΤΡ·ΜΗΤ.

Elagabalus (A.D. 218–22)

Obv. IMPCMAVPANTωNЄI (sometimes incompletely preserved). Laureate bust of Elagabalus r., draped.
Rev. PЄTΛA/COLON (sometimes partially off flan). Founder ploughing r. with bull and cow.

1373. Æ ↓ 6.64.
1374. Æ ↑ 5.52.
1375. Æ ↑ 4.15. *Obv.* !PCMAVPANTωNNOC [*sic*].
1376. Æ ← 8.28.
1377. Æ ↑ 6.13.

PHILADELPHIA

Local (Pompeian) era beginning 64/3 B.C.

Quasi-Autonomous

Obv. ΦΙΛΑΔΕΛΦΕωΝ Veiled bust of Demeter l.; behind shoulder, torch; to r., countermark: bearded male bust r.
Rev. Bundle of five ears of grain; above ...ΕΜ.... The date is not clear. Similar coins regularly have ΓΜ/LΡ (A.D. 80/1). See Sp., p. 245, no. 1.

1378. Æ ↑ 7.82.

Obv. ΦΙΛ·ΚΟΙ·CΥΡΙ Veiled bust of Demeter r., wearing wreath of ears of corn; in lower r., two ears of corn.
Rev. Cista mystica; to l. and r., ЄΤΟΥC SKC (A.D. 164/5).

1379. Æ ↓ 4.46.

Titus (A.D. 79–81)

Obv. ...CΚΑΙCΑΡ Laureate bust of Titus r.; on neck, countermark: bearded male bust r.
Rev. ...ΦΙΛΑ.... Laureate bust of Heracles r.

1380. Æ ↑ 12.66.
1381. Æ ↑ 10.55. Probably obv. die of 1380.
1382. Æ ↑ 11.94. Probably obv. die of 1380.

Hadrian (A.D. 117–38)

Obv. Laureate bust of Hadrian r., draped.
Rev. ΤVΧΗΦΙΛΑΔΕΛΦΕωΝΚC Bust of Tyche r.

1383. Æ ↑ 11.32. *Obv.* ΑVΤΟΚΡΑΔΡΙΑΝΟCCЄΒΑCΤΟC.

1359 1360 1361 1362 1363 1364 1365

1366 1367 1368 1369 1370 1371

1372 1373 1374 1375 1376 1377

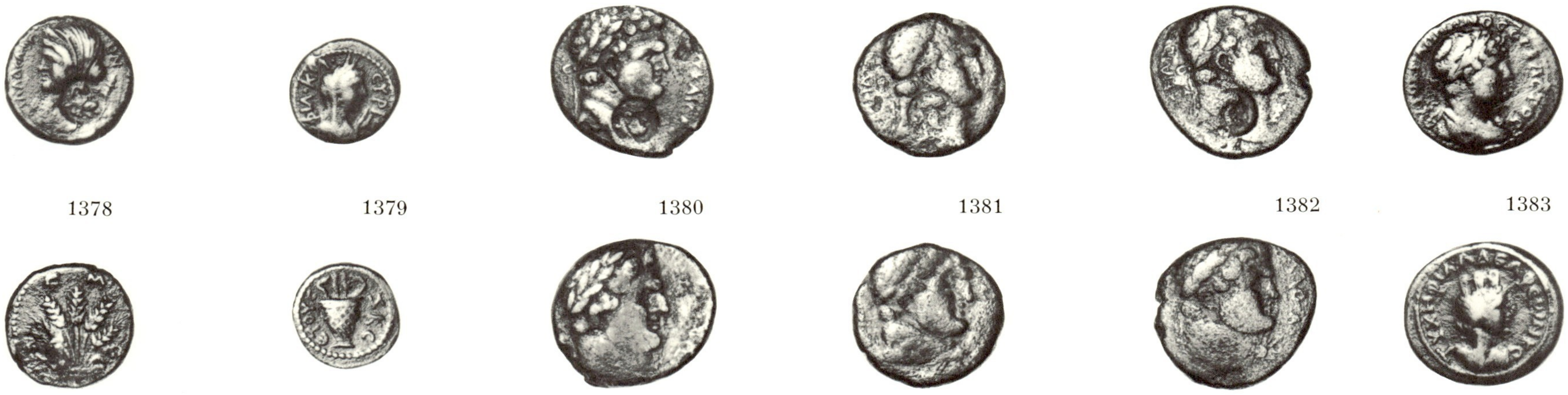

1378 1379 1380 1381 1382 1383

1384 1385 1386 1387 1388 1389

1390 1391 1392 1393 1394 1395

1396 1397 1398 1399 1400 1401

1402 1403 1404 1405 1406 1407

DECAPOLIS, ETC.: PHILADELPHIA

Hadrian (cont.)

Rev. ΦΙΛΑΔΕΛΦΕΩΝ ΚC Veiled bust of Demeter r., holding bunch of ears of corn.

1384. Æ ↑ 7.19. *Obv.* ΑΔΡΙΑΝΟCCΕΒΑCΤΟC.

Rev. ΦΙΛΑΔΕΛΦΕΩΝ ΚΟΙΛΗCCΥΡΙΑC Laureate bust of Heracles r., wearing lion skin over shoulder.

1385. Æ ↑ 10.96. Chipped. *Obv.* ΑΥΤΟΚΡΑΑΡΙΑΝΟCCΕΒΑC-ΤΟC.
1386. Æ ↑ 10.92. *Obv.* inscription as 1385.

Antoninus Pius (A.D. 138–61)

Obv. ΑΥΤΚΑΙCΑΡ ΑΝΤΩ ΝΕΙΝΟC Laureate bust of Antoninus Pius, draped.
Rev. ΦΙΛΑΔΕΛΦΕΩΝ ΚΟΙΛCΥΡΙΑC Bust of Heracles r., wearing lion skin over shoulder.

1387. Æ ↓ 8.91.

Rev. ...ΑΔΕΛΦΕΙ Tyche standing r., holding scepter and cornucopiae, resting l. foot on uncertain object.

1388. Æ ↓ 5.24. *Obv.* ΑΝΤΩΝ....

Marcus Aurelius (A.D. 161–80)

Obv. Draped bust of M. Aurelius r., laureate (1389) or radiate (1390–91).
Rev. ΦΙΛΑΔΕΛΦΕΩΝ Bust of Heracles r., wearing lion skin over shoulder.

1389. Æ ↑ 8.37. *Obv.* ΑΥΤ·ΚΑΙC·Μ·ΑΥΡ·ΑΝΤΩ....

Rev. ΦΙΛΑΔΕΛΦΕΩΝ ΚΟΙ·CΥΡ Bust of Tyche r.

1390. Æ ↓ 6.89. *Obv.* ΑΥΤ·ΚΑΙC·Μ·ΑΥΡ·ΑΝΤ·CΕ.
1391. Æ ↓ 8.06. *Obv.* inscription as 1390.

Lucius Verus (A.D. 161–69)

Obv. ΑΥΤ·ΚΑΙC·Λ·ΑΥΡ·ΟΥΗΡΟC Laureate bust of L. Verus r., draped.
Rev. ΦΙΛ·ΚΟΙ·CΥΡΙ·ΘΕΑΑCΤΕΡΙΑ Veiled bust of Asteria r.; over head, star.

1392. Æ ↖ 13.16.
1393. Æ ↑ 11.96. *Obv.* die of 1392.

Rev. ΦΙΛΑΔΕΛΦΕΩΝ ΚΟΙΛΗCCΥΡΙΑC Laureate bust of Heracles r., wearing lion skin over shoulder.

1394. Æ ↑ 9.02.

Commodus as Caesar (A.D. 177–80)

Obv. Λ·ΑΥΡ·ΚΟΜ ΜΟΔΟCΚΑΙC (incompletely preserved). Draped bust of young Commodus r.
Rev. ΦΙΛ·Κ·CΥΡ·ΘΕΑΑCΤΕΡΙ Veiled bust of Asteria r.; over head, star.

1395. Æ ↓ 6.42.
1396. Æ ↓ 8.77. Edge damaged. *Obv.* die of 1395.

Commodus as Emperor (A.D. 180–92)

Obv. ΑΥΤΚΛΑΥ.... Laureate bust of Commodus r.
Rev. ΦΙΛ·Κ·C·ΗΡΑΚΛΙΟΝ.... Domed canopy on chariot drawn by four horses.

1397. Æ ↑ 15.16.

Elagabalus (A.D. 218–22)

Obv. ΑΥΚΕCΑΡΑΝΤΟΝΙΝΟ (sometimes incompletely preserved). Laureate bust of Elagabalus r., draped.
Rev. ...CΥΡ.... Domed canopy on chariot drawn by four horses; above, countermark: club.

1398. Æ ← 7.79.

Rev. ΦΙΛΚΟΙCΥΡ Veiled bust of Asteria r.; over head, star.

1399. Æ ↗ 2.59.
1400. Æ ↗ 3.43. *Rev.*. die of 1399.
1401. Æ ↑ 2.53.

PHILIPPOPOLIS

Divus Marinus

Obv. ΘΕΩΜΑΡΙΝΩ Bust of Marinus r., supported by eagle r.
Rev. ΦΙΛΙΠΠΟΠΟΛΙΤ ΩΝΚΟΛΩΝΙΑC Roma standing l., holding phiale and spear; in lower r., shield; to l. and r., S C.

1402. Æ ↑ 6.34.

Philip I (A.D. 244–49)

Obv. ΑΥΤΟΚΚΜΙΟΥΛΙΦΙΛΙΠΠΟCCΕΒ Draped bust of Philip I r., laureate.
Rev. ΦΙΛΙΠΠΟΠΟΛΙΤΩΝ ΚΟΛΩΝΙΑC Roma seated l., holding eagle supporting two small figures (Dioscuri) and spear; in lower r., shield; to l. and r. S C.

1403. Æ ↓ 18.91.
1404. Æ ↓ 16.68.
1405. Æ ↑ 16.15.

Rev. Inscription as 1403. Roma standing l., holding phiale and spear; in lower r., shield; to l. and r., S C.

1406. Æ ↓ 7.60.

Otacilia Severa

Obv. ΜΑΡΩΤΑCΙΛΙCΕΥΗΡΑΝCΕΒ Draped bust of O. Severa r.
Rev. ΦΙΛΙΠΠΟΠΟΛΙΤΩΝ ΚΟΛΩΝΙΑC Roma seated l., holding eagle supporting two small figures (Dioscuri) and spear; in lower r., shield; to l. and r., S C.

1407. Æ ↓ 14.63.

DECAPOLIS, ETC.: PHILIPPOPOLIS (cont.)

Philip II (A.D. 247–49)

Obv. ΑΥΤΟΚΚΜΙΟΥΛΙΦΙΛΙΠΠΟCCΕΒ Draped bust of Philip II r., radiate (1408–9), or laureate (1410–12).
Rev. ΦΙΛΙΠΠΟΠΟΛΙΤΩΝ ΚΟΛΩΝΙΑC Roma seated l., holding eagle supporting two small figures (Dioscuri) and spear; in lower r., shield; to l. and r., S C.

1408. Æ ↓ 13.70.
1409. Æ ↓ 13.52. Holed. Probably obv. die of 1408.
1410. Æ ↑ 17.26.
1411. Æ ↑ 16.60.

Rev. Inscription as 1408. Roma standing l., holding phiale and spear; in lower r., shield; to l. and r., S C.

1412. Æ ↓ 7.73.

RABBATHMOBA

Local era beginning A.D. 106, founding of Provincia Arabia.

Septimius Severus (A.D. 193–211)

Obv. ΑΥΤΚΑΙΛCΕΠCΕVΗΡ.... Laureate bust of S. Severus r.
Rev. ΡΑΒΒΑΘΜΩ Tyche standing r., holding scepter and uncertain object, resting l. foot on river god.

1413. Æ ↓ 7.14.

Rev. Inscription as 1413. War god (Ares, Ariel) standing facing on base, holding sword and spear with shield.

1414. Æ ↓ 14.84. *Obv.* ΑΥΤΚΑΙΛCΕΠ.

Julia Domna

Obv. ΙΟVΛΙΑ ΔΟΜΝΑ Draped bust of J. Domna r.
Rev. ΡΑΒΒΑΘ ΜΩΒΩΝ Bust of Tyche r.; below, to l. and r., Ρ Є (A.D. 210/1).

1415. Æ ↑ 14.12.

Rev. ΡΑΒΒΑΘ ΜΩΒΑ War god standing facing, holding sword and spear with shield; flanked by two torches (or flaming altars); to l., ΡЄ (A.D. 210/1).

1416. Æ ↑ 16.09. *Obv.* die of 1415.
1417. Æ ↑ 12.28. Probably obv. die of 1415.

Geta (A.D. 209–12)

Obv. ΑVΤΚΠ· ΠΓЄΤΑC Laureate bust of Geta r., draped.
Rev. ΡΑΒΑΘ ΜUΒΑ War god standing facing, holding sword and spear with shield; flanked by two torches (or flaming altars).

1418. Æ ↓ 14.27.

Rev. ΡΑΒ...ΘΜΩΒΩΝ Poseidon standing l., holding dolphin and trident, resting r. foot on prow; to l. and r.; Ρ Δ (A.D. 209/10).

1419. Æ ↘ 8.54.

Elagabalus (A.D. 218–22)

Obv. ΑV·ΚЄCΑΡΑΝ .... Laureate bust of Elagabalus r.
Rev. ΑΡCΑ[ΠΟΛΙC] (retrograde). Poseidon standing l., holding dolphin and trident, resting r. foot on prow.

1420. Æ ↑ 8.18.

E. NABATAEAN COINS: DAMASCUS

Newell references are to the individual coins in E. T. Newell, *Late Seleucid Mints in Ake-Ptolemais and Damascus*, NNM 84 (New York, 1939).

Aretas III (84–71 B.C.)

Obv. Diademed head of Aretas III r.
Rev. ΒΑΣΙΛΕΩΣ/ΑΡΕΤΟΥ/ΦΙΛΕ ΛΛΗΝΟΣ Tyche of Damascus seated l. on rock, holding cornucopiae; below, river god; to l., ΑΡ.

1421. Æ ↗ 6.67. Newell 146λ.
1422. Æ ↗ 5.92. *Obv.* die of 1421. Newell 146κ.
1423. Æ ↗ 7.02.
1424. Æ ↗ 6.75.

PETRA (REQEM)

Meshorer references are to the individual coins in Y. Meshorer, *Nabataean Coins*, *Qedem* 3 (Jerusalem, 1975).

Obodas II (62–60 B.C.)

Obv. Diademed head of Obodas II r.
Rev. Nabataean inscription

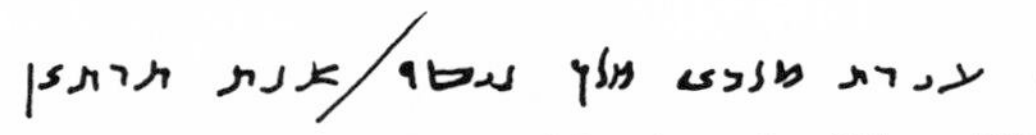 = ʿBDT MLKʾ MLK NBṬW (Obodas the King, King of the Nabataeans). Eagle standing l.; from r. to l., ŠNT TRTYN, year two (61 B.C.).

Half shekel.

1425. AR ↑ 6.25. *BMCArabia*, p. xii, pl. 49, 2 (this coin).

Syllaeus (9 B.C.)

Obv. Diademed head of Obodas III r.; to l., Š(S[yllaeus]).
Rev. Two cornucopiae crossed; between horns, Š.

1426. Æ ↑ 2.56.

Aretas IV (9 B.C.–A.D. 40)

Obv. Aretas IV, head diademed (1427) or bust laureate (1428–33).
Rev. ...ŠNT ʾRBʿ, year four (6/5 B.C.). Female figure (wife of Aretas IV, Huldu ?) standing l.; to l. and r., O H.

1427. Æ ↑ 4.12. *Obv.* to l. and r. H O.

Rev. Two cornucopiae crossed; between horns, X "4" (6/5 B.C.).

1428. Æ ↑ 1.97. *Obv.* to l. and r., O H.

Rev. 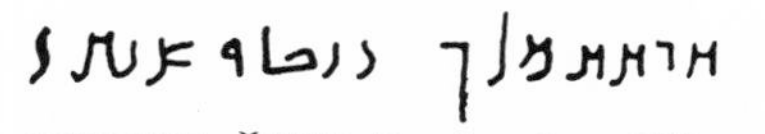 = ḤRTT MLK NBṬW ŠNT 5, Aretas King of the Nabataeans, year 5 (5/4 B.C.). Type as 1427: to l. and r., O H.

1429. Æ ↑ 4.86. *Obv.* to l. and r., H O.

Rev. Two cornucopiae, parallel; to r., PS (Phas[ael]).

1430. Æ ↑ 1.95. *Obv.* as 1428.

Rev. Type as 1428.

1431. Æ → 1.47. *Obv.* to r., H (Ḥ). *Rev.* between horns, PS.
1432. Æ ↑ 1.38. *Obv.* illegible. *Rev.* between horns, H (monogram of Aretas).
1433. Æ ↑ 2.19. *Rev.* as 1428; between horns O; at junction of cornucopiae, H (Ḥ). Meshorer 74.

Obv. H within laurel wreath.
Rev. Eagle standing l.; to r., H (Ḥ).

1434. Æ ↑ 1.52.

Obv. Aretas IV, laureate, standing l., holding spear (off flan) and sword in scabbard; to r., H.
Rev. Shuqailat, Aretas' second wife, standing l.; to l., wreath; to r., ...Q... (ŠQYLT).

1435. Æ ↑ 2.42.

1408 1409 1410 1411 1412

1413 1414 1415 1416 1417 1418

1419

1420

1421 1422 1423 1424 1425 1426 1427

1428 1429 1430 1431 1432 1433 1434 1435

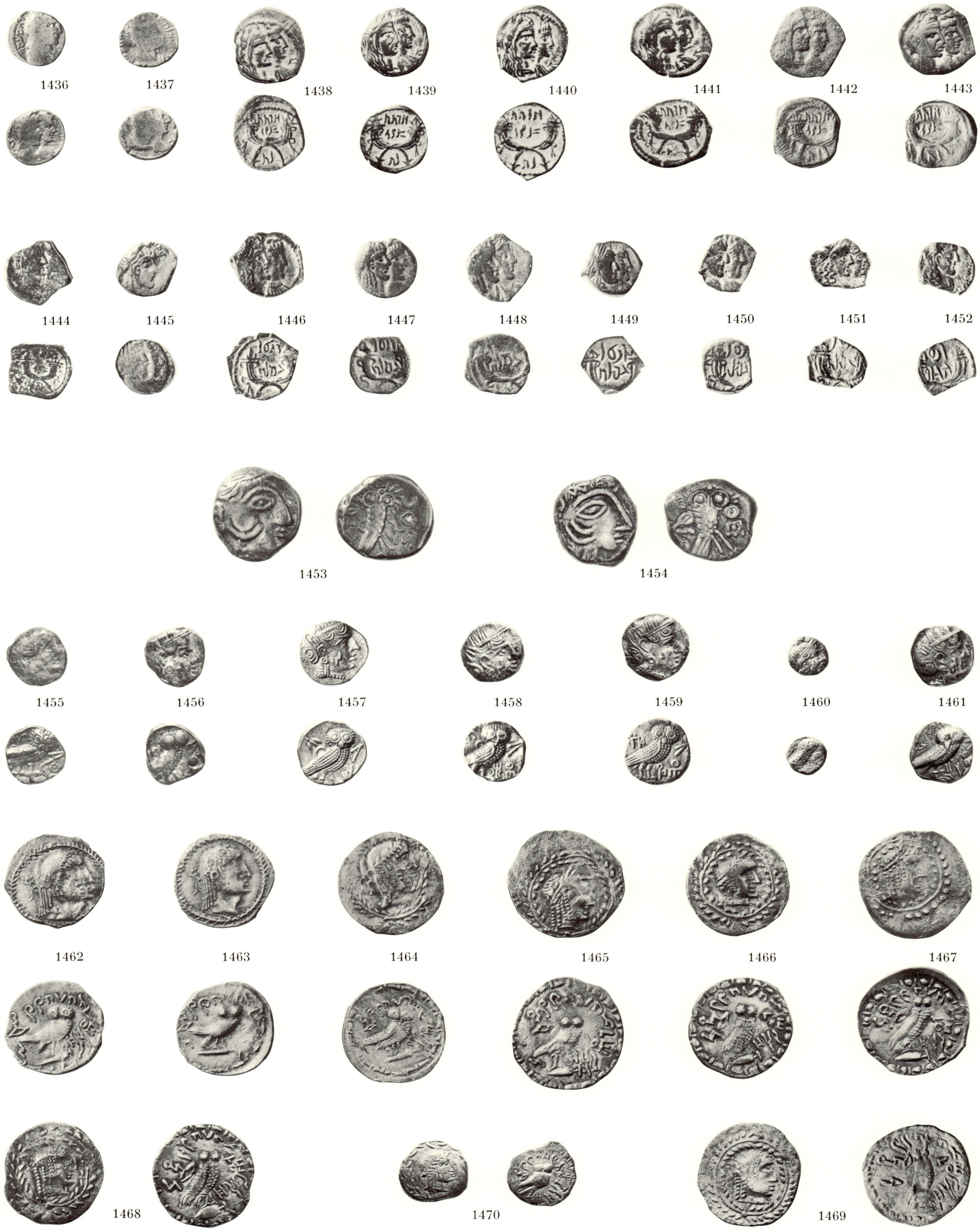

1436 1437 1438 1439 1440 1441 1442 1443

1444 1445 1446 1447 1448 1449 1450 1451 1452

1453 1454

1455 1456 1457 1458 1459 1460 1461

1462 1463 1464 1465 1466 1467

1468 1470 1469

NABATAEAN COINS: PETRA

Aretas IV (cont.)

Obv. Nabataean inscription 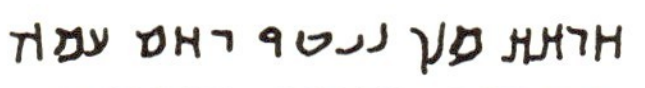 (partially preserved) = ḤRTT MLK NBṬW RḤM ʿMH (Aretas, King of the Nabataeans, the lover of his people). Laureate bust of Aretas IV r., draped.
Rev. Nabataean inscription  = ŠQYLTMLKTNBṬWŠNT (Shuqailat Queen of the Nabataeans, year). Jugate busts of Aretas IV, laureate, and Shuqailat, draped.
Denomination uncertain.

1436. AR ↑ 3.70. *Rev.*  = year 34 (A.D. 25/6).
1437. AR ↑ 3.87. *Rev.*  = year 37 (A.D. 28/9).

Obv. Jugate busts of Aretas and Shuqailat r.; to l. and r., H Š (mostly off flan).
Rev. Nabataean inscription 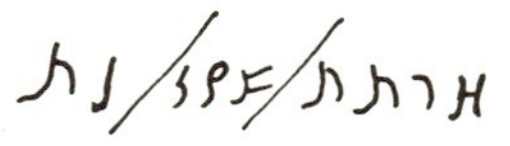 = ḤRTT/ŠQY/LT (Aretas Shuqailat). Type as 1428.

1438. Æ ↑ 5.34.
1439. Æ ↑ 3.89.
1440. Æ ↑ 4.28.
1441. Æ ↑ 3.83.
1442. Æ ↑ 4.46.
1443. Æ ↑ 3.62.

Malichus II (A.D. 40–70)

Obv. Jugate heads of Malichus II and his wife, Shuqailat II, r., laureate.
Rev. Nabataean inscription 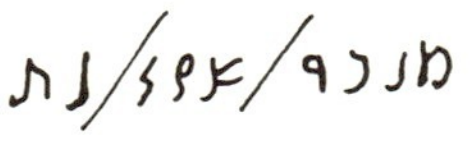 = MLḴW/ŠQY/LT (Malichus Shuqailat). Two cornucopiae crossed.

1444. Æ ↗ 2.81.

Rabbel II (A.D. 70–106)

Obv. Nabataean inscription 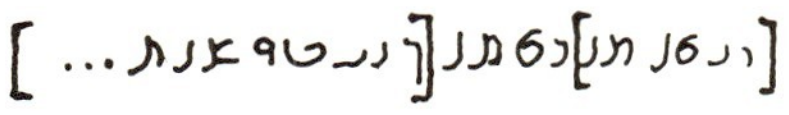 = [RB'L ML]K' ML [Ḵ NBṬWŠNT...] (Rabbel the King, King of the Nabataeans, year...). Laureate bust of Rabbel II r.
Rev. Nabataean inscription  = GMLT 'Ḥ[TH MLKT NBṬW] (Gamilat, his sister, Queen of the Nabataeans). Veiled head of Gamilat, Rabbel's wife, r.
Denomination uncertain.

1445. AR ↑ 3.30.

Obv. Jugate head of Rabbel II and Gamilat r., laureate.
Rev. Nabataean inscription 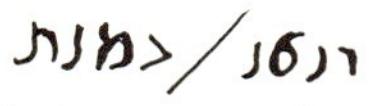 = RB'L/GMLT (Rabbel Gamilat) between horns of two cornucopiae crossed.

1446. Æ ↑ 2.97.
1447. Æ ↑ 3.24.
1448. Æ ↖ 2.38.
1449. Æ ↑ 2.86. Different style of inscription. Meshorer 163a.
1450. Æ ↑ 2.88.
1451. Æ ↑ 2.24.

Obv. Jugate busts of Rabbel II and his second wife, Hagru, r., laureate.
Rev. Nabataean inscription 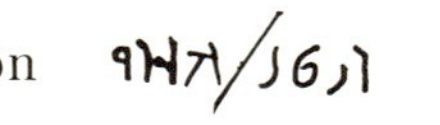 = RB'L/HGRW (Rabbel Hagru). Type as 1446.

1452. Æ ↑ 2.96.

F. SOUTH ARABIAN COINS

Imitations of Athenian Tetradrachms (Third cent B.C. ?)

Obv. Head of Athena r.; very crude style.
Rev. Owl standing r., face frontal; on l., olive sprig.

1453. Æ ← 12.78. *Rev.* downward to r., ƆΘE.
1454. Æ ← 13.80. *Rev.* downward to r., ѱ ΘE.

SOUTH ARABIA FELIX: SABAEANS

(Third cent. B.C.)

Obv. Head of Athena r., wearing crested helmet adorned with olive leaves; on cheek, ɴ (N).
Rev. Owl standing r., face frontal; to l., olive sprig.
Denominations uncertain: units (1455–59), fraction (1460)?

1455. AR ↘ 4.80. *Rev.* to r., AΘE.
1456. AR ↓ 4.36. *Rev.* as 1455.
1457. AR ↓ 5.42. *Rev.* to r., A[DH]. *BMCArabia*, p. 50, no. 54 (this coin).
1458. AR ↓ 4.87. *Rev.* to r., ΛΘE; in lower r.,  = HMR (mint of Hamir?). Naville 5, 18 June 1923 (BM dupls.), 2004.
1459. AR ↓ 5.45. *Rev.* as 1458, but in lower r.,  reversed = YD. Naville 5, 18 June 1923 (BM dupls.), 2007.
1460. AR ↓ 1.17. *Obv.* on cheek, T. *Rev.* to r., A.

Time of Shahar-Hilal (end of second cent. B.C.)

Obv. as 1455.
Rev. Sabaean inscription  = D̲H A⊙E [ŠHR] HLL [YN]P̲ (Shahar-Hilal, the exalted). Type as 1455.
Unit.

1461. AR ↓ 5.42. Naville 5, 18 June 1923 (BM. dupls.), 2003.

HIMYARITES—KATABANIANS

No further information is available at the ANS concerning the Sanʿa Hoard of 1879 and the Ma'rib (Aden) Hoard of 1921 and the Axum Hoard of 1970?, cited below. See Schlumberger, *Le Trésor de San'â* (Paris, 1880). As stated by G. F. Hill, in *BMCArabia*, p. xlv, Ma'rib was the capital of the Sabaean tribe.

Imitations Of "New Style" Athenian Tetradrachms

(End of second cent. to first cent. B.C.)

With the Name of Shahar-Hilal

Obv. Oriental male head r., laureate, within wreathed border.
Rev. Himyarite inscription

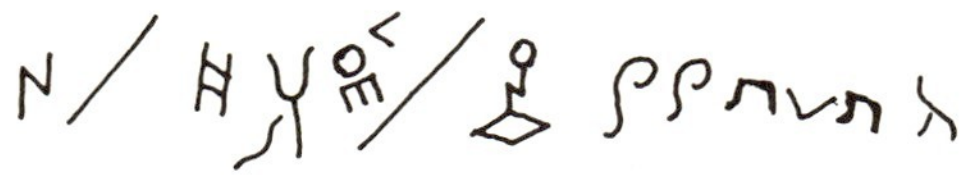

=A⊙E/SHR HLL (the king's name in Liḥyanite), YNP̲ ("exalted", the king's title in Sabaean), HD̲R (probably minted at Ḥaḏhûr, east of Sanʿa = Liḥyanite), N (Sabaean letter). Owl standing r. on amphora.

Units.

1462. AR → 5.56. Sanʿa Hoard of 1879.
1463. AR ← 5.53. Sanʿa Hoard of 1879.
1464. AR ↘ 5.41. Sanʿa Hoard of 1879.
1465. AR ↑ 5.42. Sanʿa Hoard of 1879.
1466. AR → 5.39. Sanʿa Hoard of 1879.
1467. AR → 5.46. Sanʿa Hoard of 1879.
1468. AR ↑ 5.43.
1469. AR ← 4.95.
1470. AR ↙ 2.63. Half unit. *Rev.* no letter N.

SOUTH ARABIAN COINS: HIMYARITES (cont.)

1471. Æ ← 5.32. As 1462, but obv. head l. San'a Hoard of 1879.
1472. Æ ← 5.26. As 1471. San'a Hoard of 1879.

With Monograms Only

Obv. Type l. as 1471 (1473–74), or r. as 1462 (1475–84).
Rev. Type as 1462. To l. and r., monograms; in r.,  .

Denominations uncertain. Units (1473–78), half units (1479–81), quarter units (1482–83), one-eighth unit (1484).

1473. Æ ↘ 5.52. *Rev.* to l.,  ; to r.,  ; and or  ; below amphora, Sabaean letter N. Hamburger, 12 June 1930, 461.
1474. Æ ↓ 5.36. As 1473. San'a Hoard of 1879.
1475. Æ ↘ 5.48. *Rev.* to l., , below Sabaean letter N: to r.,  . San'a Hoard of 1879.
1476. Æ ↖ 5.49. As 1475.
1477. Æ → 5.48. As 1475. San'a Hoard of 1879.
1478. Æ ↘ 5.46. As 1475.
1479. Æ ↓ 2.62. As 1475. San'a Hoard of 1879.
1480. Æ ↓ 2.70. As 1475. San'a Hoard of 1879.
1481. Æ ↓ 2.73. As 1475.
1482. Æ ↓ 1.39. As 1475, but to l., below monogram, Sabaean letter T. San'a Hoard of 1879.
1483. Æ ↓ 1.15. As 1482.
1484. Æ ↑ 0.41. As 1475, but no single letter visible to l.

Obv. Male head l. within circular dotted border.
Rev. Inscription illegible. Owl standing r. on amphora; to l.,  ; to r.,  .

Obol?

1485. AV → 0.54. Cahn 60, 2 July 1928, 1106.

With Head of Augustus and Monograms

Obv. Imitation of head of Augustus r. (1486–94, 1497–1502), or l. (1495–96); behind head, the letter N; all within wreathed border.
Rev. Type as 1462. To l. and r., monograms.
Denominations uncertain. Units (1486–90), half units (1491–96), quarter units (1497–1502).

1486. Æ ↓ 5.42. *Rev.* to l.,  ; to r.,  .
1487. Æ ↓ 5.46. As 1486, but rev. to r.,  .
1488. Æ ↓ 5.52. As 1487. San'a Hoard of 1879.
1489. Æ ↑ 5.39. As 1487. San'a Hoard of 1879.
1490. Æ ↓ 5.43. As 1487.
1491. Æ ↓ 2.72. As 1487. San'a Hoard of 1879.
1492. Æ ↓ 2.71. As 1487. San'a Hoard of 1879.
1493. Æ ↓ 2.75. As 1487. San'a Hoard of 1879.
1494. Æ → 2.72. As 1486. San'a Hoard of 1879.
1495. Æ ↓ 2.70. As 1486. San'a Hoard of 1879..
1496. Æ ↓ 2.78. As 1486. San'a Hoard of 1879.
1497. Æ ↓ 1.37. As 1487. San'a Hoard of 1879.
1498. Æ ↓ 1.55. As 1487.

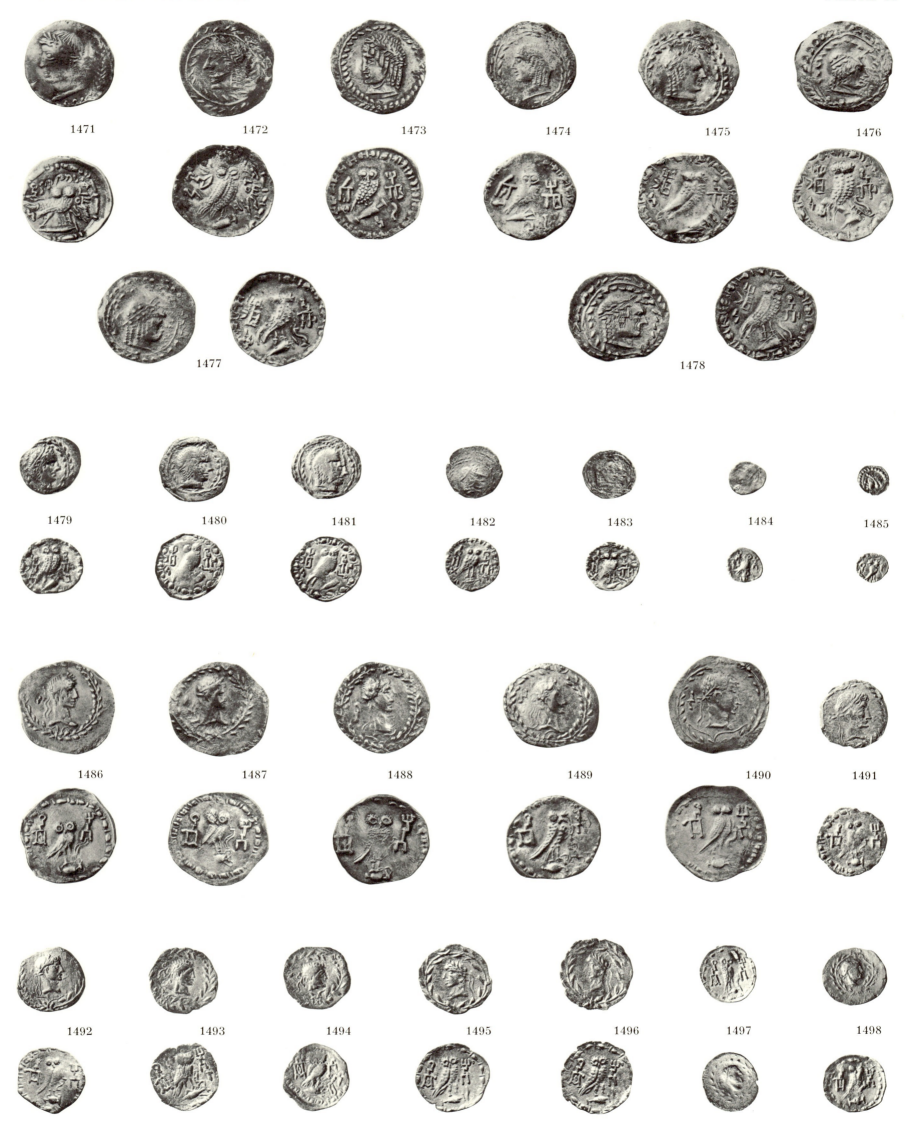

1471 1472 1473 1474 1475 1476

1477 1478

1479 1480 1481 1482 1483 1484 1485

1486 1487 1488 1489 1490 1491

1492 1493 1494 1495 1496 1497 1498

1499 1500 1501 1502

1503 1504 1505 1506 1507 1508 1509 1510

1511 1512 1513 1514 1515 1516 1517 1518

1519 1520 1521 1522 1523 1524 1525 1526

1527 1528 1529 1530 1531 1532 1533 1534

SOUTH ARABIAN COINS: HIMYARITES (cont.)

1499. Æ → 1.36. As 1487. San'a Hoard of 1879.
1500. Æ ↓ 1.25. As 1487. San'a Hoard of 1879.
1501. Æ ↓ 1.39. As 1487. San'a Hoard of 1879.
1502. Æ ↓ 1.36. As 1487.

Series with Bucranium (first cent. B.C.)

Obv. Diademed male head l.; to l., ; to r.,  ; all within circular dotted border interrupted above by crescent containing pellet (star?).
Rev. Bucranium with antelope's horns and plumes between them; to l.,  ; to r.,  ; all within circular border of two vertical lines alternating with one pellet, interrupted above by crescent containing pellet (star?).

Light denarii.

1503. Æ ↖ 3.14. Ma'rib Hoard of 1921.
1504. Æ ↑ 2.91. *Obv.* die of 1503.
1505. Æ ↑ 2.96. *Obv.* die of 1503.
1506. Æ ↑ 2.66. Ma'rib Hoard of 1921.
1507. Æ ↘ 3.48. Ma'rib Hoard of 1921.
1508. Æ ↘ 2.98.
1509. Æ ← 2.80.
1510. Æ ↖ 2.59.
1511. Æ → 3.09.
1512. Æ ← 3.09. *Obv.* die of 1511.
1513. Æ → 2.94. Ma'rib Hoard of 1921.
1514. Æ ↑ 3.07. Ma'rib Hoard of 1921.
1515. Æ ↙ 2.94. Ma'rib Hoard of 1921.
1516. Æ → 3.11.
1517. Æ ↓ 2.83.
1518. Æ ↓ 3.12.
1519. Æ ↗ 3.17.
1520. Æ ↓ 3.32.
1521. Æ → 2.89.
1522. Æ ↖ 2.93. *Obv.* sign to r. missing.

Obv. Similar to 1503, but no crescent above.
Rev. Similar to 1503, but no crescent above; to l.,  or  .

Denominations uncertain.

1523. Æ ↑ 4.04. Ma'rib Hoard of 1921.
1524. Æ ↘ 2.82. Ma'rib Hoard of 1921.
1525. Æ ↓ 2.94.
1526. Æ ← 3.13.
1527. Æ ↓ 2.91.
1528. Æ → 3.22.
1529. Æ ↑ 2.49.
1530. Æ ↑ 2.96. Ma'rib Hoard of 1921.

Obv. Similar to 1523, but to r.,  .

Rev. Type as 1523, but to l.,  ; to r.,  .

Denominations uncertain.

1531. Æ → 2.80.
1532. Æ ↗ 2.54.
1533. Æ → 2.89.
1534. Æ ↘ 2.97. *Obv.* die of 1533.

SOUTH ARABIAN COINS: HIMYARITES (cont.)

1535. AR → 2.86.
1536. AR ↑ 2.52. Ma'rib Hoard of 1921.
1537. AR ↓ 3.00. Ma'rib Hoard of 1921.
1538. AR → 3.06. *Obv.* die of 1537.
1539. AR → 3.31.
1540. AR → 2.96. *Obv.* die of 1539. Ma'rib Hoard of 1921.
1541. AR → 2.73. Ma'rib Hoard of 1921.
1542. AR ↘ 2.89. *Obv.* die of 1541. Ma'rib Hoard of 1921.
1543. AR ↑ 2.73.
1544. AR → 3.04.
1545. AR ↗ 2.97.
1546. AR ↑ 3.18. *Obv.* to r., .
1547. AR → 2.46. As 1546.
1548. AR ↓ 2.82. As 1546.
1549. AR → 2.83. *Obv.* to r., .

Obv. Type as 1523, but to l., ; to r., .

Rev. Type as 1523, but to l., ; to r., .

Denominations uncertain.

1550. AR ← 3.03. Ma'rib Hoard of 1921.
1551. AR ↓ 2.98. Ma'rib Hoard of 1921.
1552. AR ← 2.92. Ma'rib Hoard of 1921.
1553. AR ← 3.07. Ma'rib Hoard of 1921.

Obv. Type similar to 1523, but head r.; to l., ; to r., .

Rev. Type as 1523, but to l., ; to r., .

1554. AR ← 2.72. Ma'rib Hoard of 1921.
1555. AR ← 2.44. Ma'rib Hoard of 1921.
1556. AR ↖ 2.94. Ma'rib Hoard of 1921.

The following nos. 1557–73 are crude Himyarite copies.

Obv. Male head r., probably type as 1503.
Rev. Bucranium, type as 1503.

1557. Æ → 0.99. *Rev.* to l., ; to r., . Axum Hoard of 1970 (?).
1558. Æ ← 0.69. Probably as 1557.
1559. Æ ↓ 0.53. Probably as 1557.
1560. Æ ↖ 0.34. Probably as 1557.
1561. Æ ↙ 0.26. Probably as 1557. Axum Hoard of 1970 (?).
1562. Æ → 0.10. Probably as 1557.
1563. Æ ← 0.36. Similar to 1557, but obv. head l.; to l., .
1564. Æ ↑ 0.49. *Obv.* to r., traces of letter M (?). Axum Hoard of 1970 (?).
1565. Æ → 0.60. *Rev.* to l., ; to r., . Axum Hoard of 1970 (?).
1566. Æ ↗ 0.57. Probably as 1557.
1567. Æ → 0.74. Probably as 1557.
1568. Æ ↘ 0.25. Probably as 1557. Axum Hoard of 1970 (?).
1569. Æ ← 0.19. Probably as 1557.
1570. Æ ↖ 0.39. *Obv.* to r., . Axum Hoard of 1970 (?).
1571. Æ ↓ 0.61. *Obv.* above, small crescent and pellet (star?).
1572. Æ → 0.75. *Obv.* to l., letter Ḥ?
1573. Æ ↓ 0.28. *Obv.* type as 1571; to l. and r., unclear signs. *Rev.* Uncertain type, either very crude bucranium or bird.

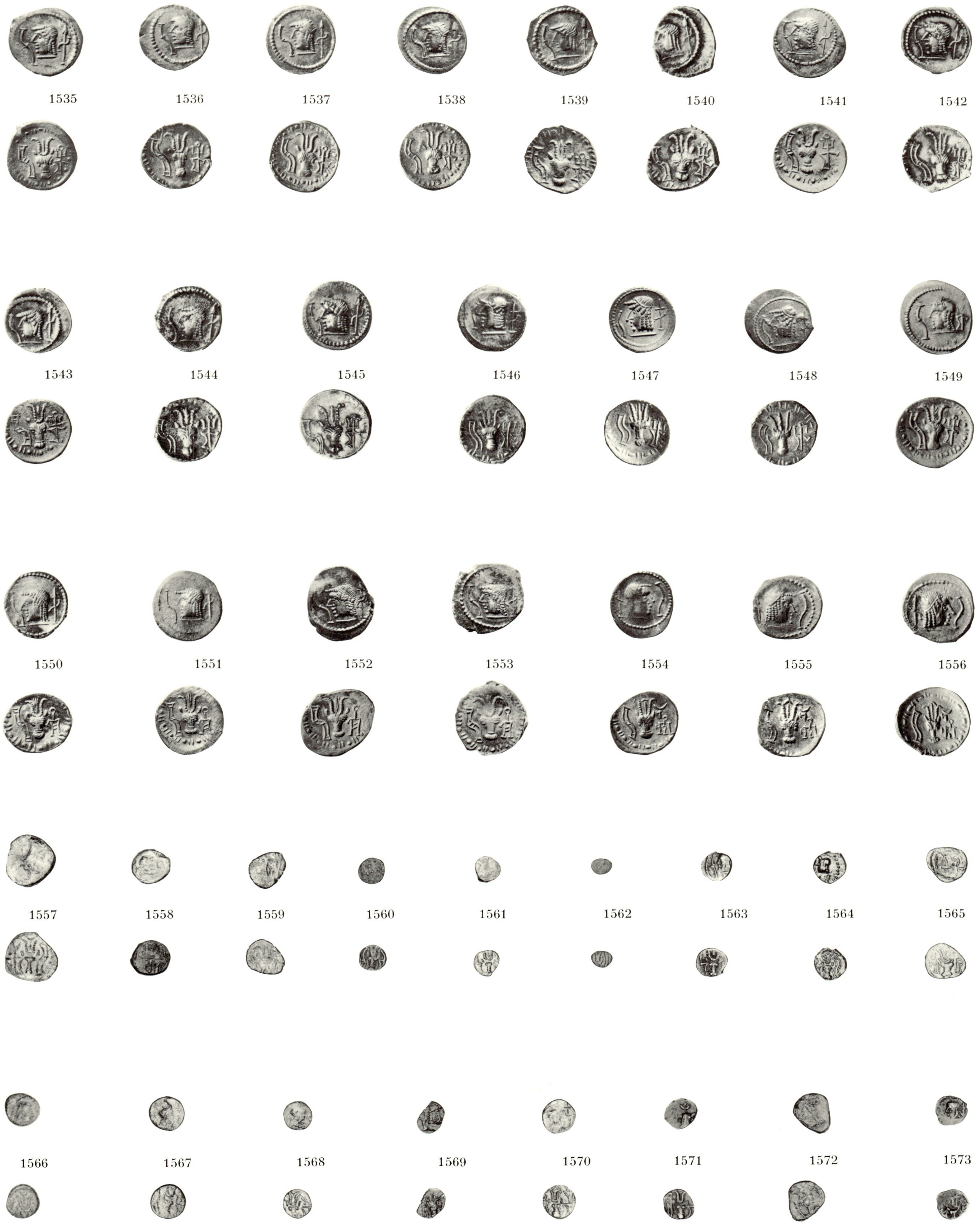
1535 1536 1537 1538 1539 1540 1541 1542
1543 1544 1545 1546 1547 1548 1549
1550 1551 1552 1553 1554 1555 1556
1557 1558 1559 1560 1561 1562 1563 1564 1565
1566 1567 1568 1569 1570 1571 1572 1573

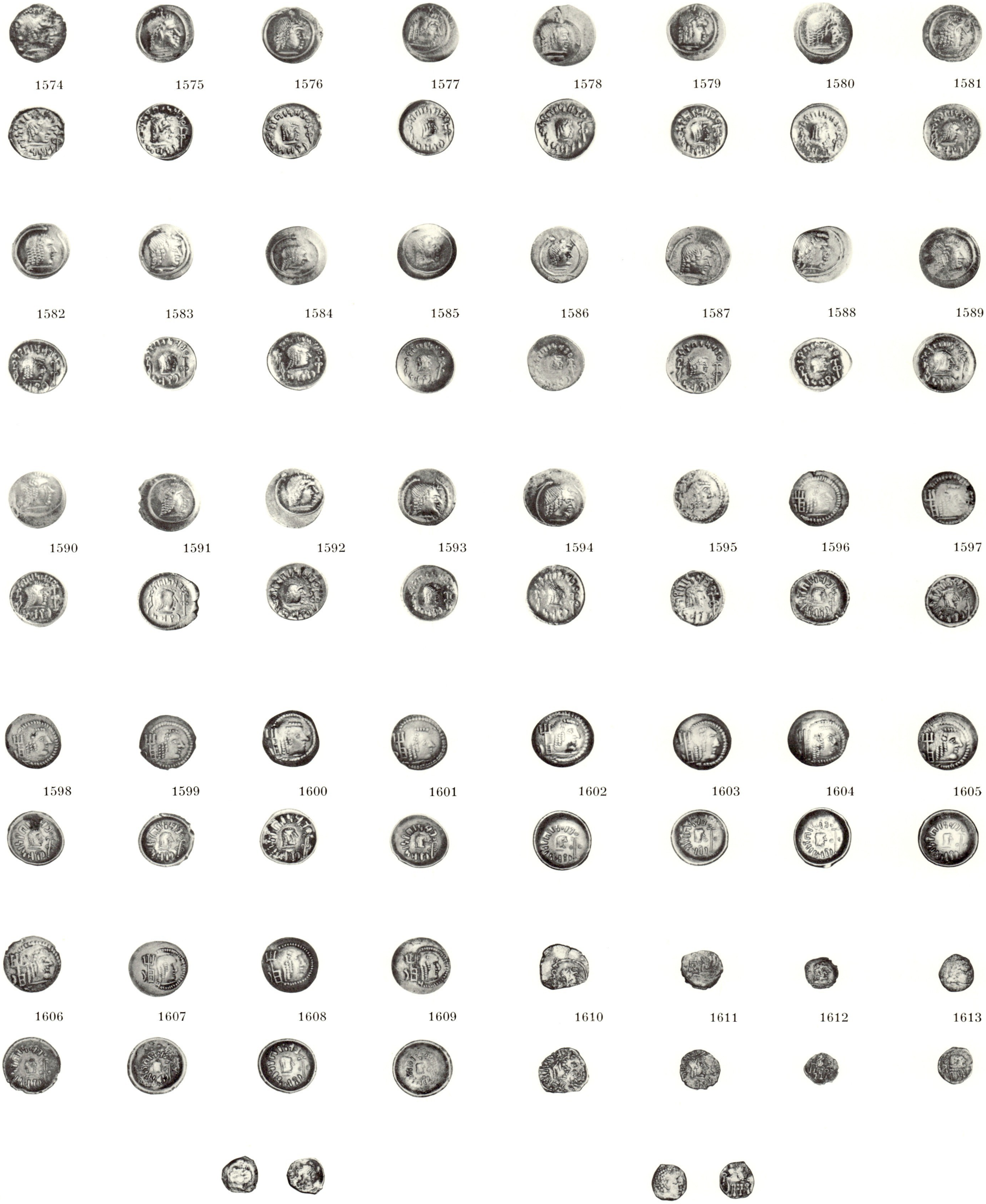

1574 1575 1576 1577 1578 1579 1580 1581

1582 1583 1584 1585 1586 1587 1588 1589

1590 1591 1592 1593 1594 1595 1596 1597

1598 1599 1600 1601 1602 1603 1604 1605

1606 1607 1608 1609 1610 1611 1612 1613

1614 1615

SOUTH ARABIAN COINS: HIMYARITES (cont.)

RAIDAN

Silver, Usually Scyphate (A.D. 50–150)

Under Karib'il Yehun ʿim Wattar

Obv. Male head r.; headdress with ringlets on neck; hair bound with taenia (or wreath?); to l., (Wattar).
Rev. Sabaean inscription = KRB'L YHNʿM/RYDN. Small male head r.; to l., ; to r., or .

Light half denarius.

1574. Æ ↑ 1.25.

Under ʿamdan Bayyin (*Yanaf*)

Obv. Male head r., laureate, surrounded by a penannular torc; above, the letter Y.
Rev. Sabaean inscription = ʿMDN BYN (YNP̱ in monogram) / RYDN. Small male head r.; to r., or .

Light half denarii.

1575. Æ ↓ 1.58.
1576. Æ ↓ 1.50.
1577. Æ ← 1.39.
1578. Æ ← 1.46.
1579. Æ ↑ 1.79.
1580. Æ ↑ 1.67.
1581. Æ ↗ 1.56. *Obv.* no letter Y.
1582. Æ ↑ 1.59.
1583. Æ ↗ 1.52.
1584. Æ ↓ 1.63.
1585. Æ ↑ 1.64.
1586. Æ ↖ 1.56.
1587. Æ ↑ 1.44.
1588. Æ ← 1.23.
1589. Æ ↓ 1.90.
1590. Æ ← 1.57.
1591. Æ ↖ 1.40.
1592. Æ → 1.95.
1593. Æ ↓ 1.75.
1594. Æ → 1.78.

Under ʿamdan Bayyin (*without Yanaf*)

Obv. Head r. as 1575; to l., ; all within circular dotted border.
Rev. Sabaean inscription = ʿMDN BYN/RYDN. Type as 1575; to r., or .

Light half denarii.

1595. Æ ↗ 1.87.
1596. Æ ↘ 1.06.
1597. Æ ↑ 1.70.
1598. Æ → 1.36.
1599. Æ → 1.66.
1600. Æ ↑ 1.42.
1601. Æ ← 1.18.

Rev. to r., .

1602. Æ → 1.62.
1603. Æ ↑ 1.86.
1604. Æ → 1.40.
1605. Æ ↓ 1.82.
1606. Æ ↓ 1.61.
1607. Æ → 1.58.
1608. Æ ← 1.67.
1609. Æ ↘ 1.65.

Obv. Type as 1575; to l., .

Rev. Type as 1575; to l., or .

Light quarter denarii.

1610. Æ ↑ 0.97.
1611. Æ ↑ 0.71.

Without King's Name

Obv. Type as 1595; to l., .

Rev. Type as 1575; to l., or ; below, mint name RYDN (Raidan).

Unit uncertain.

1612. Æ ↓ 0.18.

Probably under Yed''b (*Katabania*)

Obv. Male head r.
Rev. Small male head r.

1613. Æ ↑ 0.38. *Rev.* to l., (YD['ʿB]); below, mint name ḤRB (Ḥarb).
1614. Æ ↑ 0.33. As 1613.
1615. Æ ↑ 0.38. *Rev.* to l. letter Y (Yed'ʿb?); below, mint name YHBR (Yehabir).

INDICES

1. GEOGRAPHICAL

2. RULERS, PRINCES AND GOVERNORS